THE MERITOCRATIC INTELLECT

Studies in the History of Educational Research

THE MERITOCRATIC INTELLECT

Studies in the History of Educational Research

edited by
James V Smith
David Hamilton

ABERDEEN UNIVERSITY PRESS

First published 1980
Aberdeen University Press
A Member of the Pergamon Group

British Library Cataloguing in Publication Data
Seminar on the Scientific Movement in Educational Research, *University of Aberdeen, 1979*
The meritocratic intellect.
1. Educational research—Congresses
I. Title
II. Smith, James V
III. Hamilton, David, *b. 1943*
370'.78 LB1028

ISBN 0 08 025720 8

Typescript by Mrs S Fell

PRINTED IN GREAT BRITAIN AT
ABERDEEN UNIVERSITY PRESS

CONTENTS

EDITORS' NOTE

The papers in this volume derive from a seminar on 'The Scientific Movement in Educational Research' organised by the Scottish History of Education Society and sponsored by the Social Science Research Council. The Seminar was held at the University of Aberdeen in September 1979. It commemorated the one hundredth anniversary of the publication of Alexander Bain's *Education as a Science*. Bain was Professor of Logic and English at Aberdeen from 1860 to 1880 and, among other things, wrote a biography of James Mill, collaborated with John Stuart Mill, and founded the journal *Mind* in which the term 'mental test' was used for the first time.

INTRODUCTION

Donald J. Withrington
Director, Centre for Scottish Studies, University of Aberdeen
Chairman, Scottish History of Education Society

It is particularly appropriate that this conference, devoted to the study of the development of education as an academic and 'scientific' discipline, should be held in Aberdeen. But before I elaborate on that topic, let me just welcome you all, not only to the University of Aberdeen but also to a meeting that is being held under the auspices of the Scottish History of Education Society.

That society, a 'small but respectable body' as was once remarked about the Episcopal Church in Scotland, has newly passed its first ten years of existence. During that time it has drawn much strength from a deliberately eclectic approach to the history of Scottish and others' education. We pride ourselves on not being narrowly or professionally oriented, on treating the subject with the flexibility and expansiveness of approach that it deserves (and too seldom gets) and on attracting into our membership a wide conspectus of differing occupations and expertise - academics and research students albeit, but leavened by journalists and publishers, schoolteachers and HM inspectors, and a goodly representation of 'independent scholars', by no means all to be categorized as 'educationists' but rather as social and economic or administrative historians, as sociologists, as philosophers or psychologists, benefitting from the variety of viewpoints which our meetings demonstrate.

Today, we embark on something rather different - a residential conference drawing speakers from the USA as well as from the UK; but the subject-matter of our meeting, and the varied approaches to its common theme which are indicated in the lecture-titles, are well within the terms of our ten-year-old tradition. Welcome to Scotland, therefore, to our visitors; and welcome into the friendly and yet challenging atmosphere of our Society's meetings. And welcome still more, to the university which in 1860 - as it celebrated at last the unification of the two ancient colleges and universities of King's in Old Aberdeen and Marischal in New Aberdeen - called to the new chair of Logic in the united university the illustrious Alexander Bain, author of the frequently-reprinted and widely-translated _Education as a Science_.

For Bain the twin principles of _utility_ and _order_ were everything, themselves a reflection of the continued strength of 18th-century Enlightenment thought in Aberdeen. His antagonism to the continuing predominance of classics, in schools and universities, and his barely-concealed distaste for organised religion and certainly for a state-supported religious faith, epitomised the man. He had been taught himself in the Aberdeen tradition of the Scottish common sense school of of philosophy, and in many respects remained a natural scientist who turned his hand after 1860 to the rigorous teaching of English - mainly rhetoric, very little literature - and to an exposition of Logic which was dominated by his associationist psychology, firmly based on physiology. In his works on education we find evidence of both of these influences: a searching after accessible principles, ordered into an easily-grasped methodological synthesis, concise and clear and direct, and avoiding what he conceived to be unnecessary elaboration or complexity; and a strong natural science base to it all - education was a specifically applied discipline which grew out of the 'parent sciences' of mathematics, physics, chemistry and physiology by way of philosophy, one which was formed and shaped by them and was to be elucidated through them.

But it is not my place to elaborate on this theme, in any way to 'steal the clothes' of speakers whom you are still to hear, better informed than I am. I merely remind you of the aptness of choosing Aberdeen for this meeting. But I might add one thing: Bain was not perhaps, in Aberdeen or in Scotland, quite so novel in his general philosophical or language teaching or even in his approach to educational studies, as has sometimes been claimed. What he did, essentially, was to bring his analysis into the forefront, not least in promoting the study of education as 'foremost among the applied sciences ... the subject of the day ... the most feasible and hopeful of the practical applications of conjoined psychology and logic'. But he was, nonetheless, very much a part of that long-standing tradition of philosophical-psychological and natural history studies in Aberdeen which had its roots in mid-18th century. Indeed, almost immediately after graduating, Bain had remained at Marischal College in the 1840s to teach moral philosophy and then natural philosophy; he then taught mathematics as a professor at the Andersonian College in Glasgow before moving to London as assistant secretary to the Metropolitan Sanitary Commission and then at the General Board of Health; latterly he was also examiner in philosophy for the University of London and also for the Indian Civil Service examinations. This seemingly wayward 'progress' towards the Aberdeen chair in Logic was typical enough of the time. After all, just before Bain returned to Aberdeen in 1860, a professor of Divinity who had been teaching at Marischal College in Bain's earlier days there - William Robertson Pirie - and who had been unsuccessful in his attempts to obtain the Logic chair in 1846, was 'converted' in the united university into professor of Church History: and Pirie in 1858 published a prize essay which was held to 'cover the whole province of psychology, traversed with practical intent, repudiating all interest in metaphysics', An Inquiry into the Constitution, Powers and Processes of the Human Mind, with a View to the Determination of the Fundamental Principles of Religious, Moral and Political Science.

No matter, it seemed, what stipend-bringing disciplines were then proposed in Aberdeen, the scientific study of the learning and teaching processes and the organization of education in which they could flourish were in the forefront of attention in this city. That perennial topic is before us again, and I hope Aberdeen once more provides fruitful ground for its examination.

EDUCATIONAL RESEARCH AND THE SHADOW OF JOHN STUART MILL

David Hamilton
Lecturer, Department of Education
University of Glasgow

ABSTRACT

This paper examines the origins, logic and impact of the methodological synthesis performed by John Stuart Mill in the 1830s. It is well known that Mill's philosophical ideas were important to the subsequent development of pragmatism, progressivism and fabianism. Perhaps less well known, however, is that the self-same beliefs also had a formative influence upon the development of a constellation of methodological techniques that include regression analysis, analysis of variance and random sampling.

****

> There cannot be a worse authority in any branch of political science than of merely practical men. They are always the most obstinate and presumptious of theorists! (J.S. Mill)[1]

Since at least the Second World War a key component of the advanced training of educationists has been the provision of courses in research design and methodology. One consequence of such a development is that 'methodology' has become separated from other areas of educational enquiry. In turn, 'research' has gained popular acceptance as an instrumental activity - merely the application of recipe knowledge.

More recently, however, the technological view of educational research has come under close scrutiny.[2] Nevertheless, much of the discussion is still pitched at the level of methodology. Solutions are sought merely in the form of 'better' or 'alternative' recipes. The superordinate status of method is tacitly accepted; the assumptions that support its hegemony are left unscrutinised.

This paper attempts to recover some of the innocence of educational enquiry. It argues that the work of John Stuart Mill (1816-1883) played a formative role in the creation of 20th century scientism. Writing at a time when the boundaries of the social sciences (and indeed their names) were still under review, Mill pulled together a diverse set of ideas that reached back through James Mill (1773-1826) and Jeremy Bentham (1748-1832) to Adam Smith (1723-1790) and Isaac Newton (1642-1727).

In the process, he created a vigorous school of social thought that, in its turn, reached forward through Karl Pearson (1857-1936) and William James (1842-1910) to Edward Thorndike (1874-1949) and Ronald Fisher (1890-1962).

It is well known that Mill's ideas were an important source for the major 20th century social credos of pragmatism and fabianism.[3] Perhaps less well known, however, is the fact that a supposedly ethically- and ideologically-neutral constellation of methodological techniques (e.g. regression analysis, analysis of variance and random sampling) can be traced back to the self-same notions.[4]

By the dawn of the 20th century the primary colours used to shade the world map of western knowledge had already been chosen. Although parts of the map have since been painted over, Mill's initial writings remain important in two respects. First, they give access to some of the epistomological leaps (or breaks) that went into the early formulation of western social science methodology; and second, they offer one explanation as to the long-term survival of such ideas.

From an historical perspective, then, this essay is about John Stuart Mill's contribution to the formative years of the social sciences. At a more general level, it is also a case study in the articulation of ideology and methodology. The body of this paper contains a concise review of Mill's ideas and influence. The notes - which can be read separately - provide a qualifying yet supportive counterpoint.

Mill and the Philosophic Radicals

John Stuart Mill's mother was the daughter of a London asylum-keeper. His father was a Scots-born, free-lance author. Mill was educated at home by his parents and, vicariously, by his father's friends who included the philosopher Jeremy Bentham, the economist David Ricardo and the radical Francis Place. At the age of fourteen he spent a year in France and, three years later, began a life-long career in the London Headquarters of the East India Company. Mill's work at India House allowed him considerable free time such that in the 1820s he was able to make his mark, politically, socially and philosophically, in a series of articles for the Westminster Review (founded by Bentham in 1823) in the London Debating Society and in the Utilitarian Society (founded by Mill in 1823). Mill's academic originality dates from the late 1820s - a period also associated with his active work in support of parliamentary reform.

As a young man, John Stuart Mill espoused the cause of philosophic radicalism - a philosophical standpoint that was a direct expression of the dual industrial and political revolutions that disrupted Europe and North America in the late 18th and early 19th centuries. Typically, philosophic radicals supported the interest of the upwardly mobile industrial capitalists against the more conservative views of the hitherto ascendant landed classes. Their consequent rejection of a static view of society went hand-in-hand with a wide range of reforming policies directed towards the realignment of political and industrial life.

Collectively, if not individually, philosophic radicals shared a related and overlapping set of self-evident (or 'natural') beliefs. They assumed, like the revolutionaries of the period, that all men are created equal (thus preferring social divisions in society to be based on merit rather than birth). They adopted a materialist sense-psychology (believing that knowledge is conditioned more by experience than by the innate properties of mind). They believed that the worth of social policies, like the efficiency of a machine, could be rationally calculated (and not simply deemed a matter of faith). And finally, like their non-conformist call for freedom of worship, the philosophical radicals agitated for the freedom of the market place (regarding free trade as a more effective source of national improvement than the protectionist economic policies of the landed producers and the trading monopolies).[5]

The coherence of philosophic radicalism

Despite their varied provenance, the elementary propositions of philosophic radicalism had certain points of internal contact. Ideas about the mind were linked to notions about human conduct which, in turn, were linked to assumptions about moral and economic policy.

The psychological basis of philosophic radicalism was provided by associationism - a theory of knowledge harking back to Locke (1632-1704) and Bacon (1561-1626). Associationism assumed, first, that mental images were a reflection of external stimuli and, second, that association (or contiguity) of different external objects helped to create the internal (i.e. mental) association of the images of such objects. (If, for instance, the mind learns the concepts 'sweetness' and 'honey' at the same time, associationism argues that the recollection of 'honey' will also cause the mind to resonate with the sensation of 'sweetness'. Similarly, experience of 'jam' would also lead, via the association 'sweetness', to the idea of 'honey'). By such chaining procedures associationism could account for the gradual creation of an educated mind out of a series of initially independent (or atomistic) external sensations.

From a theory of sensation, philosophic radicalism moved easily into the realm of ethics. It assumed that certain sensations - notably those that create pleasurable effects - are sought out by humans in preference to those which create pain. Further, since philosphic radicals believed that pleasure-seeking was a 'natural' propensity (and therefore common to all members of the human species), they could also assume that all humans were drawn, in common, to the same pleasures.

By positing such a shared 'identity of human interests', the philosophic radicals bridged the gap between individual psychology and collective ethics. Since they held that all humans share the same scale of values, they could quite legitimately compute the aggregate level of pleasure in society by 'adding up' the pleasurable (or painful) increments created by the actions of individuals. Thereafter, it was only a small step to propose that 'correct' social policies were those which increased the aggregate level of societal satisfaction.

The identity of interests assumption also spilled over into the economic theories of philosophic radicalism. The corner stone of classical economics - the freedom of the market place - was justified in philosophic radical terms on the basis that buyers and sellers benefit to the same degree (i.e. share an identity of interest) in the exchange process. Further, philosophic radicalism argued, by the same token, that the trading actions of individuals would, at the aggregate level, also enhance the collective fortunes (or common wealth) of the human species - guiding it 'progressively' along the road to eternal happiness.

Mill's Utilitarian Synthesis

During the 1830s, Mill, a second generation philosophic radical, took the foregoing ideas even further. He explicitly set out to bring to matters of government the same precision and consensus that could be obtained in astronomy. He believed that, given such an achievement, the moral (i.e. social and political) sciences would achieve parity with the physical sciences. Mill worked for over ten years on the problem - with outstanding success. His labours, which contributed to 'the most productive (period) in the history of English thought on method',[6] transformed a corpus of ideas into a system of thought, an ideology into a science. He gave philosophic radicalism a new thrust, a new name (utilitarianism) and a new manifesto (A System of Logic, 1843).[7] Recently, the final section of A System of Logic has been described as 'the most enduring essay on the method of the social sciences which has ever been written'.[8]

Set against the standards of the 18th century Enlightenment, Mill's contribution in the 1830s was not so much philosophical as methodological. He took the ideas of medieval logic and combined them with more recent notions about the analysis of sense experience. Mill believed that A System of Logic was a natural (and thus non-controversial) science of nature and society that could be placed at the service of social policy making. As both the 'father of systematic empiricism'[9] and the 'godfather of English liberalism'[10] Mill's parentage and patronage were as profound as they were far-reaching.

In Mill's own words, A System of Logic provided the 'links of thought' necessary to 'cement together' the pre-existing 'true portions of discordant theories'.[11] To strengthen his ideas, however, Mill introduced some new ingredients. First he advanced the claim that logic should embrace inductive as well as deductive operations. Like Francis Bacon's Novum Organum (1620), Mill's Logic argued that the theory and practice of science should incorporate observations (inductive) as well as logical (deductive) elements - on the grounds that the former were the ultimate source of new knowledge. (Both Bacon and Mill regarded deduction as the mere restatement of truths already embedded in the initial premises of the syllogism).

In the early 19th century most philosophers followed Hume and took a sceptical position on induction. Mill stalled these indeterminancy objections (e.g. the sun may not rise tomorrow) with the covering law that nature is uniform in time and space (e.g. on the basis of our experience the sun will rise tomorrow). The uniformity of nature principle, then, rescued the problem of induction and, at the same time, raised it to the same level of certainty as deductive logic. By his re-analysis of induction, Mill created a 'larger logic'[12] which, in its acceptance of both empirical (i.e. inductive) and mental (i.e. deductive) operations, offered a more comprehensive account of human intellectual activity.[13]

Mill's second contribution brought inductive reasoning even closer to formal logic. He explicated a series of methodological procedures - analogous to the syllogistic rules of logic - which could establish and test inferences derived from observation. Following Newton, Mill believed that an important purpose of science was to disentangle the simple causal mechanisms (or 'single facts') which, taken together, create the world of observed effects.[14] Mill's experimental 'canons' - the methods of 'agreement', 'difference', 'residues' and 'concomitant variation'[15] were a milestone in the codification of the experimental method.[16] Each one described a different sequence of logical and empirical manipulations (i.e. 'varying the circumstances')[17] by which means the 'general' atomic causes could be differentiated from the plurality of 'partial'[18] causes.

Having outlined a set of maxims appropriate to empirical enquiry in general, Mill then focuses on some of the issues specific to the moral sciences (e.g. questions of freedom, necessity, consciousness). In 'On the logic of the moral sciences' Mill advanced two controversial claims. First, that the moral and natural sciences lie on the same methodological continuum. And second, that the basic laws of the moral sciences are psychological not social.[19] In the first case he argued against the view that the moral sciences lie beyond the realm of the natural sciences; and in the second instance, he argued against the view - largely associated with Comte (1798-1857) - that the laws of human nature could be derived from the phenomena of history.

To argue against historicists like Comte, Mill differentiated between empirical and causal laws. The former, he held, are only approximate statements about human nature, whereas causal laws are exact and universal. Thus, Mill believed that observationally-based (i.e. empirical) laws of human society have no independent status; they are merely an expression of more deeply-rooted 'psychological and ethological laws' governing 'the action of circumstances on men and of men on circumstances'.[20] Whereas Comte gave priority to history, Mill gave priority to human (or 'natural') propensities.

Mill's adherence to a natural science model of human behaviour did not add up to an acceptence of mechanical determinism. Rather, Mill believed that a science of society should primarily be concerned with behaviour at the aggregate level - where 'general' (but not 'partial') causes operate to shape the common future of the human race.

For Mill, the theoretical distinction between 'partial' and 'general' causes was not problematic. Indeed, it was not regarded as a theoretical issue at all - merely a matter of measurement:

> Whenever it is sufficient to know how the great majority of the human race of some nation or class of persons will think, feel and act, these propositions are equivalent to universal ones. For the purpose of political and social science this <u>is</u> sufficient. [21]

Whatever the merits of the individual assumptions of utilitarianism, their internal coherence gave Mill's system considerable practical momentum. Ironically, the net social impact of Mill's reductionist philosophy of science proved much greater than the sum of its parts (for which, individually, Mill claimed no originality).[22] The internal harmony of Mill's ideology also provided the basis of its long-term survival. Despite piece-meal attack, the entire system survived. Its momentum turned into inertia as successive generations accepted its assumptions without reflection.

To summarise: Mill's system of logic and morality was built round four cornerstones - the identity of human interests, the uniformity of nature, the primacy of psychological constructs, and the methodological equivalence of the physical and moral sciences. The elements of Mill's thought were inter-related and knowable - just like the motion of the planetary spheres. Collectively, they enabled Mill and his followers to move easily, if unconsciously, between the realms of psychology, political action, morality and scientific practice. Although Mill was, himself, aware of the provisionality of his thought - he wrote <u>A System of Logic</u>, not <u>The System of Logic</u> - his ideas eventually broke from their epistemological moorings. In due course, his powerful synthesis was drawn even more tightly upon itself. Coherence became closure and, for more than a century, Western social science recast itself from the same unyielding mould. Shorn of its social and philosophical context, and isolated by the internal divisions of 20th century intellectual labour, Mill's 'general logic of scientific enquiry'[23] was transformed into a technology as unquestionably accepted as it was vigorously applied.[24]

In such a context, Mill's supreme achievement, perhaps, was to secure his own disappearance from the methodological consciousness of subsequent generations. Compared with other theoreticians like Marx, Durkheim and Weber, Mill's name is neither identified with any exemplary empirical investigation, nor, as in the case of Pearson or Fisher, commemorated in any widely-used statistical test. Like the assumptions which acted as midwife to his method, Mill has become an un-noticed guest at his own celebration. But however modest his fame, his influence has been without rival.[25]

Mill's Methodological Testament

As suggested, the substance and tenor of A System of Logic has had a formative influence on the course of Western social science. Its arguments regarding the aims, organisation and conduct of science have achieved normative status. That is, it began as one among several major philosophies of enquiry, but in time, became the only accepted philosophy of science. A System of Logic set a standard against which all others were to be judged - a role which, unacknowledged, it still performs.

For instance, the notion that research is a mere fact-gathering exercise harks back to Mill's primary concern for the elucidation of summary facts (which he preferred to call empirical laws). Indeed, insofar as Mill deemed facts to be 'things'[26] he also believed that they could be readily classified and enumerated. The consequent analysis of empirical data was envisaged as taking a reductionist form: observational summaries were to be further condensed until they could be described in terms of causal psychological laws. Mill paid little attention to the role of theory in the identification and categorisation of facts since, for him, there was only one relevant organising theory - his own.[27]

Mill's reductionist strategy necessarily followed from his initial assumptions. As noted earlier, he regarded empirical laws merely as surrogate expressions of more fundamental natural (and causal) laws. Mill's dominant concern with the reduction of data was a stimulus for much of the early development of statistical practice - particularly insofar as early statisticians shared Mill's views about the natural (i.e. innate) basis of human action. Equally, Mill's views about the priority of 'Laws of Mind'[28] does much to explain the subsequent domination of psychological forms of reasoning and theorising within education.

Mill's belief that laws could be 'read off' directly from empirical generalisations necessarily forestalled discussion of alternative explanations. Mill's analyses always focused on ill-fitting data, never ill-fitting theory. He believed, in effect, that he had gone beyond theory - that there was no longer any need to consider the merits of rival standpoints. Unwittingly, therefore, he assumed the consensus that A System of Logic set out to establish. Mill's procedure for establishing laws from observation - the 'inverse deductive method'[29] - would be unexceptionable if, in use, it were not so one-sided. Mill always deferred to psychological reasoning. Empirical laws were always to be validated against (unobservable) principles of human nature. Discussing the possibility of erroneous generalisations, Mill wrote that 'the only check or corrective is, constant verification by (sic) psychological and ethological laws'.[30]

In practice, Mill's methods tended to support the status quo: anomalous data were rejected as erroneous; or explained away in terms of the 'diversities of local circumstances'.[31] Mill's joint recourse to psychological explanation and to the uniformity of nature was, therefore, not only inherently conservative, it also vitiated his claim that utilitarianism was a philosophy of 'experience'.[32]

Besides its general influence on the entire structure of Western scientific practice, Mill's espousal of psychological forms of explanation had a range of more specific consequences. Following the (then) Newtonian model of the physical sciences, Mill believed that the basic elements of human thought and behaviour operated and interacted as discrete, mutually-independent social forces. Such 'billiard-ball' viewpoints foreshadowed accounts of social behaviour whereby the net effect is deemed to be created by the additive influence of the elemental forces.[33] In Mill's case, such a view also fitted well with the individualistic and additive assumptions that underpinned the ethical calculus of utilitarianism. Towards the end of the 19th century it also provided a secure philosophical basis for the development of regression analysis (which embodies the same assumptions about the independent and additive interaction of variables) and, more generally, the 'hypothetico-deductive method'.[34]

Mill's preference for biological forms of explanation was also reflected in his use of the individual as the basic unit of social analysis (cf. the category of the atom in chemistry). The practice of 'methodological individualism' (as it came to be known) had considerable practical and policy implications. Given the associated assumption of an identity of interest, it under-wrote, first,the aggregation of individual behaviour (deeming the net effect to be the sum of the individual effects) and, second, it supported the notion that, by a reverse process, the combined effect could be used as a basis for making prescriptions about individual conduct (assuming, as it were, that what is good for the average is also good for the individual).[35]

Mill's strategy was perfectly reasonable but it did rely upon the prior belief that society is a 'social organism' held together by a 'consensus' of its 'different parts'.[36] Methodological individualism not only supports a biological and consensus view of society (viz. all parts of the social body are in harmony and agreement with each other), it also bolsters formal sampling theory. The latter relies upon an assumption that all members of a given sample and population share the same attributes, just as it relies on the uniformity of nature assumption to legitimise the extrapolation from sample to population. Without these atomistic assumptions about the uniformity of nature and the identity of human interests, sampling theory would look rather different.[37]

As might be anticipated, Mill's view gave substantial support to Social Darwinism - the belief that human history is a continuous extension of animal evolution. In the wake of Darwin's revelations, social Darwinism accepted not only the methodological but also the theoretical unity of the social and natural sciences - synthesis which had a formative influence on the post-Darwinian study of mental or psychometric attributes.

Psychometry, like its parent activity anthropometry, was influenced by Quetelet's (1796-1874) earlier claim that physical attributes are distributed among the population according to a Gaussian (i.e. bell-shaped) curve. As shown elsewhere, the founding father of psychometry, Francis Galton (1822-1911), took Quetelet's claim as proven and extended it to the psychometric domain.[38] Further, Galton guaranteed the 'truth' of Quetelet's 'law' in a manner derived from Mill. When confronted with measures that did not fit the normal curve (e.g. those that produced a bimodal distribution) Galton confidently rejected them on the grounds (furnished by Darwin (1809-1882)) that such signs of discontinuous variation indicated the presence of more than one type (species, race, etc.). Galton's use (or misuse) of Mill's 'inverse deductive method' transformed Quetelet's hypothesis into a law and allowed the Gaussian distribution to be relabelled (by Galton) as the 'normal' curve.[39] If nothing else, Galton's sponsorship (and Cyril Burt's stewardship) of the normal curve probably stands as the most visible testimony to the normative power of Mill's logic.

Just as Mill's views on the additivity and independence of causes underwrote the early development of regression analysis, so they also had an impact on Ronald Fisher's formulation of analysis of variance. Mill's distinction between 'general' and 'partial' causes mirrors Fisher's distinction between 'treatment' and 'local' causes of variability.[40] Further, the conduct of analysis of variance (viz. the teasing apart of different 'causes'[41] by logical and empirical manipulation) is a direct descendant of Mill's canons of experimental investigation.[42]

Mill's consensus view of scientific enquiry accorded well with his political views. Just as he sought to achieve consensus within science, he also sought, through science, to achieve consensus in society. To adjudicate and interpret (and thereby legitimate) the results of empirical enquiry, Mill used the internalist criterion of inter-subjectivity. A statement was held to be true if judged to be so by the superior wisdom of an intellectual elite.[43] In the political context of the first half of the 19th century (when a majority of the population were without the vote) Mill believed that such an instructed minority could serve to enlighten (and civilise) the majority who remained in ignorance. That is, he hoped to achieve a society where:

> The body of the people, i.e. the uninstructed, shall entertain the same feelings of deference and submission to the authority of the instructed, in morals and politics, as they at present do in the physical sciences.[44]

In the first half of the 19th century Mill's radicalism merely extended to the replacement of the landed aristocracy by a learned aristocracy. Despite its internal conservatism, therefore, Mill's system was a powerful vehicle for the expression and validation of meritocratic and individualistic viewpoints - a characteristic which it still retains. Although Mill believed that his methods provided a 'natural' (or ethically neutral) form of social engineering, he still envisaged, like the pragmatists, fabians and liberals, that control should remain in the hands of a political minority of experts.

SUMMARY AND CONCLUSIONS

This paper has advanced five propositions. First, that modern research practice (particularly in education) is shot through with a range of invisible assumptions which not only serve to shape its practices but also to validate its outcomes. Secondly, that many of the key ideas of the present can be traced back at least as far as John Stuart Mill's A System of Logic. Thirdly, that Mill's particular contribution - a philosophical synthesis - gave a boost to the relative autonomy and survival of such ideas. Fourthly, that the power of Mill's ideas was sufficient to sustain within Western social science a belief in the value-free status of methodology. And finally, that if other reasonable assumptions had been adopted, the conduct of contemporary social science might have been rather different.

Most accounts of Mill are written by political philosophers or by philosophers of science. Few studies seem to have dwelt upon the inter-penetration of philosophy and methodology. In a sense, then, the unilateral focus of this paper upon the constituent elements and logical structure of Mill's ideas is deliberate. Nevertheless, the outcome may appear, to paraphrase Trevelyan, rather like an essay in the history of ideas with the history left out.[45] Certainly, it should be read primarily as a ground-clearing statement. Much of the social context and internal evolution of Mill's ideas has been omitted - largely because such a redefinition of the topic is beyond the author's current competence.

It might be argued, too, that this account falls foul of the genetic fallacy - implying on the one hand that Mill's views have survived unaltered until the present day; and ignoring, on the other, the contributions made by subsequent thinkers. Again the narrow focus is, in part, deliberate. For the sake of brevity the essay relies on 20th century judgements of Mill's continued influence, eschewing any attempt to produce a fully anotated intellectual genealogy (but see elsewhere in this volume).

Finally, to an educationist, much of the argument may seem negative - at best a combined essay about the thoughts of a dead philosopher and the pitfalls of systems thinking. Indeed, the essay stops short of discussing alternative views of science. Yet, in its attempt to display the problem of methodology, the foregoing discussion may be of more than historical interest.

REFERENCES

[1] J. S. Mill, Collected Works, Toronto : University of Toronto Press, 1963 onwards, Vol. 4, p. 19.

[2] Some indication of the existence and nature of the contemporary methodological debates in British educational research can be gleaned from the Presidential addresses to the British Educational Research Association. They range, chronologically, from 'Educational research : the state of the art' (John Nisbet, 1974) to 'The characteristics of educational research : mapping the domain' (Jim Eggleston, 1978).

[3] The link between Mill and pragmatism is indicated by the dedication of William James' Lectures on Pragmatism (1907) to the memory of John Stuart Mill 'whom my fancy likes to picture as our leader, were he alive today'. The links between Mill and the Fabians are well documented in Beatrice Webb's My Apprenticeship (Harmondsworth: Penguin Books, 1971). A more recent commentator has described 'fabian socialism' as a 'legitimate off-spring' of utilitarianism insofar as its 'schemes of reform' were initiated from above by the 'enlightened few for the welfare of the unenlightened many' (A. MacIntyre, A Short History of Ethics, London : Routledge & Kegan Paul, 1967, p. 238).

[4] This account rejects as ill-considered the claim that 'Most of Mill's specific contributions to the methodology of the social sciences have not had a lasting impact' (H. Magid (ed.), On the Logic of the Moral Sciences, Indianapolis : Bobbs-Merill, 1965, p. xxiv).

[5] The historical context and evolution of philosophic radical thought is detailed in E. Halevy's The Growth of Philosophic Radicalism (Boston : The Beacon Press, 1955; originally published in English in 1928).

[6] L. Lauden, 'Theories of scientific method from Plato to Mach : a bibliographic review', History of Science, 1968, 7, p. 30. Lauden specifically refers to the period 1829-1843.

[7] A System of Logic went to eight editions in Mill's lifetime. All quotations are taken from the edition that fills 960 pages of volumes 7 and 8 of the Collected Works. Further commentaries on A System of Logic, not cited elsewhere in this paper, include P. Winch, The Idea of a Social Science, London : Routledge & Kegan Paul, 1958; R. J. Halliday, John Stuart Mill, London : George Allen & Unwin, 1976; and J. M. Robson, The Improvement of Mankind : the Social and Political Thought of John Stuart Mill, Toronto : University of Toronto Press, 1968. Mill's own views on the Logic (which was initially turned down by a publisher) are reported in his Autobiography (J. Stillinger, (ed.) London : Oxford University Press, 1971, pp. 132-135).

[8] L. S. Fouer, 'John Stuart Mill as a sociologist : the unwritten ethology' in J. M. Robson and M. Laine (eds.) James and John Stuart Mill : Papers of the Centenary Conference, Toronto : University of Toronto Press, 1976, p. 86. Additional recent judgements on mill include '(the man) who had the clearest anticipatory vision of what a scientific study of man and society could be' (M. Brodbeck 'Explanation, prediction and "imperfect" knowledge', in

M. Brodbeck (ed.) Readings in the Philosophy of the Social Sciences, New York : Macmillan, 1968, p. 364); and '(A System of Logic is) one of the earliest and still perhaps the most comprehensive of all systematic positivist methodologies' (B. Hindess, Philosophy and Methodology in the Social Sciences, Hassocks, Sussex : Harvester Press, 1977, p. 117).

[9] D. Willer and J. Willer, Systematic Empiricism : Critique of a Pseudo-Science, Englewood Cliffs, New Jersey : Prentice Hall, 1973, p. 33.

[10] M. Cowling, Mill and Liberalism, Cambridge : Cambridge University Press, 1963, p. xii.

[11] Logic, preface, p. cxi.

[12] E. Nagel (ed.) John Stuart Mill's Philosophy of Scientific Method, New York : Hafner, 1950, p. xxxi.

[13] Mill described the uniformity of nature as the 'ultimate major premise' of induction (Logic, p. 308). As many critics have pointed out, the logical weakness of Mill's standpoint is that the uniformity of nature principle is, itself, an inductive inference. Further, Mill vacillates between treating the uniformity of nature assumption as a statement about nature or as a way of thinking about nature (Logic, p. 310, footnote).

[14] It may seem strange to a twentieth century reader but Mill wrote his Logic without the concept: 'variable'. Instead, he was forced to use such expressions as 'single facts' or 'simplest elements' (p. 380). Presumably, the term 'variable' grew up in the age of Charles Darwin (whose The Origin of Species (1859) might be regarded as a treatise on variability). Other related terms which took on their modern meaning around that time were 'typical' (1860) and 'average' (1830); see Oxford English Dictionary.

[15] Logic, pp. 388-406 ('Of the four methods of experimental inquiry').

[16] 'The basic structure of the experimental method has changed very little, however, from that constructed by Mill in 1843'. (D. Tiedeman, 'Experimental Method', in C. Harris (ed.) Encyclopedia of Educational Research, New York : Macmillan, 1960, p. 487).

[17] Logic, p. 381.

[18] Logic, p. 847. Mill described general causes as 'depending in the main on those circumstances and qualities which are common to all mankind' (ibid.).

[19] Mill regarded sociology (a 'convenient barbarism' for social science, Logic, p. 895) as a 'subordinate order' or 'speculation' and 'derivative' of the 'ultimate' laws of 'human nature' (Logic, p. 916).

[20] Logic, p. 914.

[21] Logic, p. 847, emphasis on original.

[22] Logic, preface, p. cxi.

[23] Logic, p. 952.

[24] The ossification of methodology is well described in the following: 'It may be said that deductivity is not a logical requirement of explanation, but a dogma of empiricist metaphysics which regards the achievements of Newton as definitive of scientific rationality. In this way, it is tied to theories of the last scientific revolution and quite unable to visualise what a new revolution in scientific thought would involve. It is the failing of empiricist metaphysics to have chained itself irrevocably to one kind of science and to have done its best to petrify scientific invention' (A. Ryan, The Philosophy of John Stuart Mill, London : Macmillan, 1970, pp. 17-18).

[25] One of the few methodological texts which explicitly acknowledges Mill's contribution is Raymond Boudon's *The Logic of Sociological Explanation* - an attempt to update the 'classical (sic) logic of John Stuart Mill' (Harmondsworth Penguin Books, 1974, p. 7).

[26] *Logic*, Book 1, chapter 3. ('Of the things denoted by names').

[27] 'Mill has nothing much to say about the role of theories in science. Because of this he talks as if the question of what the circumstances are is always to be settled by more precise inspection; he ignores the fact that the way we describe them may depend on the theory we adopt to explain them' (A. Ryan, *The Philosophy of John Stuart Mill*, London : Macmillan, 1970, pp. 10-11.

[28] *Logic*, Book 6, chapter 4.

[29] *Logic*, Book 6, chapter 10.

[30] *Logic*, p. 917.

[31] *Logic*, p. 916.

[32] 'Mine professes to be a logic of experience only', Mill to Sterling, 1839, quoted in K. Britton, *John Stuart Mill*, New York : Dover, 1969, p. 111. Mill's recourse to experience further denied any role for theory: 'Mill, trying to refer everything to "experience", has gone so far as to make experience impossible. What has dropped out of this theory is the constructive part. He substitutes for organisation combinations of disparate "things"' (L. Stephen, *The English Utilitarians*, London : Duckworth & Co., 1900, Vol. 3, p. 134).

[33] Mill was quite adamant about the discrete and additive nature of social forces: 'Men are not, when brought together, converted into another kind of substance, with different properties ... Human being in a society have no properties but those which are derived from, and may be resolved into, the laws of the nature of individual man. In social phenomena the Composition of Causes is the universal law' (*Logic*, p. 879).

[34] 'Mill's account of what it is to explain an occurrence or natural law closely resembles what is probably the most popular current account, that given in terms of the "hypothetico-deductive" model' (A. Ryan, *The Philosophy of John Stuart Mill*, London : Macmillan, 1970, p. 3).

[35] For a recent discussion of methodological individualism see Steven Lukes 'Methodological Individualism re-considered' in D. Emmet and A. MacIntyre (eds.) *Sociological Theory and Philosophical Analysis*. London : Macmillan, 1970, pp. 76-88.

[36] *Logic*, p. 918.

[37] Formal sampling theory also resonates well with liberal and pluralist ideologies. In both cases every datum or viewpoint is accorded equal weight. For a philosophical critique of formal sampling theory, see E. V. Ilyenkov, *Dialectical Logic*, Moscow : Progress Publishers, 1977, p. 344ff.

[38] D. Hamilton 'Educational Research and the shadows of Francis Galton and Ronald Fisher' in W. B. Dockrell and D. Hamilton (eds.), *Rethinking Educational Research*, London : Hodder and Stoughton, 1980, pp. 153-168.

[39] Whether Galton coined the term 'normal curve' has not, I believe, been fully established. Nevertheless, he was certainly a keen proponent of its usage.

[40] R. A. Fisher *Statistical Methods for Research Workers*, Edinburgh : Oliver and Boyd, 1954, p. 263.

[41] *Ibid.*, p. 224.

[42] The link between analysis of variance and Mill's methodological canons is made in David Tiedeman's 'Experimental Method' in C. Harris (ed.) *Encyclopedia of Educational Research*, New York : Macmillan, 1960, p. 490. The stress that Fisher placed upon the importance of randomisation is also prefigured in Mill's statement that 'that which is only probable when asserted of individual beings indiscriminately selected, being certain when affirmed of the character and collective conduct of masses' *Logic*, p. 847. It is perhaps noteworthy that pre-1851 editions of the *Logic* (1843, 1846) have a much weaker sense of randomisation. The phrase 'individual human beings indiscriminately selected' replaces the phrase 'human beings taken individually' (*Logic*, p. 847, footnote).

[43] For a critical review of the intersubjectivity criterion of truth see M. Scriven's 'Objectivity and Subjectivity in Educational Research' in L. G. Thomas (ed.) *Philosophical Redirection of Educational Research* (71st Yearbook of the National Society for the Study of Education, part I). Chicago : University of Chicago Press, 1972, pp. 92-142.

[44] *Collected Works*, Vol. 12 (*The Earlier Letters*), p. 40.

[45] G. M. Trevelyan's original aphorism was 'Social history might be defined negatively as the history of a people, with the politics left out'. See his *English Social History*, London : Longmans, Green & Co., 1944, p. vii. The difficulties and tensions encountered in writing about the relationship between the history of science and the philosophy of science have been noted elsewhere (see L. Lauden, Theories of Scientific method from Plato to Mach: a bibliographic review' History of Science, 1968, *7*, 1-63).

ALEXANDER BAIN AND THE DEVELOPMENT OF EDUCATIONAL THEORY

Walter M. Humes
Lecturer, Department of Education
University of Glasgow

ABSTRACT

This paper examines the ideas and influence of Alexander Bain (1818-1903) in the context of a discussion about the nature and development of educational theory. It is divided into four sections. In the first, a number of general questions regarding the epistemological status of educational theory are raised and related to certain broad characteristics of educational writings before and after nineteenth century developments in the sciences. Bain's career and intellectual ancestry are dealt with in the second section. The influence of J. S. Mill, Comte, Spencer and others on his philosophical thinking is considered and his characteristic method of enquiry identified. The third section looks at the consequences, both positive and negative, of Bain's application of this method to the field of education: in particular, his widely-read work Education as a Science (1879) is examined critically. In the final section, an attempt is made to assess Bain's place in the development of education as a field of study by reintroducing the broader issues raised at the start of the paper.

****

I

The precise nature of educational theory - its substance, structure and function - is highly problematic. Despite the efforts of such writers as D. J. O'Connor and Paul Hirst[1] to inject a note of philosophical rigour into attempts at definition, the essentially amorphous character of the study of education continues to reassert itself. Among the most intractable questions are these. What is the relation between educational theory and other kinds of theories - especially those which have developed in the sciences? Is educational theory primarily descriptive or explanatory or predictive or prescriptive? Does it have any kind of separate existence of its own or is it entirely parasitic on other disciplines? What is or should be the connection between theoretical formulations and the everyday practical activities of teaching and learning?

Central to all of these questions is a tension between two sets of impulses, the identification of which will be useful when viewing educational theory historically. On the one hand, there is the impulse towards precision and certainty. This is marked by attempts to achieve conceptually tight definitions of key terms, by an experimental methodology that exalts quantification, and by a pragmatic philosophy that ignores or devalues the political and ideological context of educational practice. On the other hand, there is the impulse towards completeness and what might be called experiential validity. This is marked by a distrust of attempts to define educational theory too narrowly, by a relatively loose and subjective methodology that grants more importance to values and beliefs than to data (however carefully obtained), and by a tendency to easy generalisation about the extent to which education is shaped by wider political and ideological forces. The dichotomy is, of course, a crude one - thus the wisdom of discussing the conflict in terms of impulses rather than established positions or views. It is a question of emphasis.

Nevertheless, despite this important qualification, it is instructive to ask whether this tension has always been present in educational theory or whether it is a relatively recent development. At a very general level it might indeed be possible to classify the great educators of the past as either 'rationalists' or 'humanists'[2] (to use rather unsatisfactory shorthand terms for the two sets of impulses described above). Thus Quintilian's exhaustive approach to the details of pedagogic method or Vives' detailed interest in pupil behaviour might be contrasted with the vague metaphysical values underlying the education of Plato's guardians or the all-embracing character of Rousseau's appeal to nature. But, as the example of Vives immediately suggests, this does not take one very far. And there is a very real sense in which the dichotomy I have described did not emerge with any degree of clarity until the mid-nineteenth century, with the growth of a scientific methodology under the influence of industrialisation.[3] The debate between Arnold and Huxley[4] about the true nature of a liberal education might be seen as a crucial turning point in this regard.

It might also be argued that in the pre-industrial period all educational theories had three important and inter-related features in common - features which, increasingly, have come under suspicion on 'scientific' grounds. First, educational theories were highly comprehensive in character; that is, they ranged freely over the whole domain of human experience, covering knowledge, morality, religion, social organisation, etc.. Secondly, they were unashamedly prescriptive: there is no doubt that, whatever else they were doing, writers such as Plato or Erasmus or Comenius were making recommendations about what ought to happen in education. And thirdly, educational theories were ideologically based in an open and explicit way: both Locke and Rousseau, for example, were highly conscious of the connections between their educational ideas and the structure of society. The demand which is frequently heard nowadays - to keep politics out of education - would have seemed nonsensical to them.

The present picture is radically different. In the first place, hardly any large-scale theories are on offer. It could even be argued, I think, that John Dewey's Democracy and Education (1916) represents the last significant example of that kind. Instead, what we have is a view of educational theory as consisting of a number of largely separate and highly specialized contributory disciplines - psychology, sociology, history, philosophy,[5] etc.. The question arises: is this merely a function of the growth of knowledge or does it represent a more fundamental shift? Secondly, prescription (at least in overt forms) is viewed as undesirable. As it is also inescapable (given that education must have practical outcomes), what has tended to happen is that a separation has grown up between policy makers on the one hand and educational researchers on the other. Prescription is regarded as the province of the former, thus allowing the latter to retain the illusion of academic neutrality - the extent of the illusion is worth stressing, in view of the policy constraints to which much educational research is subject. And thirdly, in so far as the ideological framework within which educational theory exists is recognized, it is regarded as a source of contamination, a messy intrusion into the realms of the pure and the value free. There are even some attempts to repudiate its relevance altogether - as in Hirst's approach to the forms of knowledge, allegedly based on logical analysis alone.[6]

The conclusion to be drawn from these observations is simply that the 'rationalist' and 'scientific'[7] impulses appear to be the dominant ones in educational theory today, just as 'metaphysical' and 'humanistic'[8] impulses were dominant prior to industrialisation. There has, inevitably, been both loss and gain in this shift and a question worth considering is whether the gains have been quite as substantial as those working within the scientific tradition often seem to suppose.

It is in the context of such issues regarding the nature and scope of educational theory that the ideas of Alexander Bain will be viewed. His Education as a Science[9] was first published exactly one hundred years ago and represents an unequivocal early statement of the merits of a scientific approach to the study of education.

II

First, some very brief and selective remarks about Bain's career and the intellectual circles he frequented are necessary to place his specifically educational contributions in perspective.[10] He was born in 1818 and graduated M. A. from Aberdeen University in 1840, taking the old general degree which included Latin, Greek, Mathematics, Natural Philosophy, Natural History, Moral Philosophy and Christian Evidences.[11] The early academic preferment which he might reasonably have expected on the basis of his record as an undergraduate did not materialize, largely because of his agnosticism, and for many years he supported himself partly by means of freelance writing covering an astonishingly wide range of subjects - scientific, historical, linguistic, philosophical, sociological.[12] He also acted for a time as Assistant Secretary to the Board of Health in London[13] and as an Examiner for London University.[14] His two principal works during this early period were The Senses and the Intellect (first published 1855)[15] and The Emotions and the Will (first published 1859),[16] both of which he revised three times. They were widely read on the Continent and in the United States and were discussed, for example, in Ribot's Psychologie Anglaise Contemporaine (1870)[17] and James's Principles of Psychology (1890).[18]

In 1860 Bain was appointed Professor of Logic at Aberdeen, a post he held with distinction for 20 years: his qualities as a teacher appear to have been considerable.[19] During this time he continued to publish at a remarkable rate, the most substantial work of this period being his two volume Logic (1870).[20] His energy and, indeed, his financial backing helped to launch the journal Mind (1876)[21] which, in its early years, published important psychological papers by, among others, Wilhelm Wundt, Francis Galton and William James.[22]

Education as a Science appeared in 1879 and, within six years, had been translated into French, German, Spanish and Italian.[23] Bain also involved himself in the educational issues of the day at a practical level as can be seen, for example, from his evidence to the 1876 Commission on the Scottish Universities[24] and from his contributions to the debates of bodies concerned with improving educational methods.[25] After his retirement his continued involvement was ensured by his election by the student body to the office of Rector of Aberdeen University in 1881 and his re-election for a second term in 1884.[26] He was particularly interested in the various plans to restructure the Arts course, a subject on which he gave evidence to the 1889 Universities Commission. According to George Davie in The Democratic Intellect, there was a feeling that Bain should in fact have been a member of the 1889 Commission, both on account of his distinction as a philosopher and teacher, and his ability to represent the Scottish tradition of general education which was under pressure from Anglicizing influences.[27]

Of greater interest than these bare facts of Bain's career are the individuals and movements whose influence helped to shape his philosophical outlook and, by extension, his approach to education. He was acquainted with a great many of the leading intellectual figures of his time, including Carlyle, J. S. Mill, Spencer, Huxley, Grote and Darwin. The connection with Mill is well-documented and can hardly be over-estimated. Mill's patronage helped to promote Bain's writings and, indeed, very early in their friendship, Mill entrusted Bain with the revision of his System of Logic. Bain made frequent visits to London throughout his career and further collaboration took place over many years.

It would be misleading, however, to say that Bain simply absorbed from Mill his empirical and utilitarian outlook and associationist psychology. Rather, he found support for many of the ideas he had already arrived at independently through private study and reflection. Furthermore, he felt confident enough to depart from Mill on a number of points and Mill himself acknowledged the independent character of Bain's thinking.[28]

Another important influence - less well-documented[29] - was certainly Auguste Comte, whose writings Bain had been introduced to by Mill and whom he actually met in 1851 during a visit to Paris.[30] In his Autobiography Bain writes: 'Comte's classification of the sciences was a wonderful advance upon anything known at the time; the three stages (theological, metaphysical, positive) being very suggestive'.[31] Positivism was discussed with considerable interest at the Aberdeen Philosophical Society of which Bain was a leading member, and in 1843 he presented a paper to the Society on the classification of the sciences based on his reading of Comte.[32] In it he found a place for psychology in Comte's hierarchy and drew a distinction between the theoretical and the practical sciences, a distinction which serves to suggest that positivism could be interpreted not only as a theory of knowledge and a scheme of history, but also as a programme of social reform. It will be argued later that, given Bain's apparent realization of this interpretation and his general support for the notion of sociology as a science, certain omissions from his treatment of education are surprising.

T. H. Huxley and Herbert Spencer must be mentioned in any account of the influences to which Bain was subject. Both are of particular interest in that they wrote extensively on education and, like Bain, argued the case for scientific education.[33] Huxley was one of his predecessors as Rector of Aberdeen University during the time when Bain was Professor of Logic there and his famous definition of a liberal education, first offered in an address of 1868, would have been entirely congenial to Bain, both in its substance and in its metaphoric language:

> That man, I think, has had a liberal education who has been so trained in youth that his body is the ready servant of his will, and does with ease and pleasure all the work that, as a mechanism, it is capable of; whose intellect is a clear, cold logic engine, with all its parts of equal strength, and in smooth working order; ready, like a steam engine, to be turned to any kind of work, and spin the gossamers as well as forge the anchors of the mind; whose mind is stored with a knowledge of the great and fundamental truths of Nature and of the laws of her operations; one who, no stunted ascetic, is full of life and fire, but whose passions are trained to come to heel by a vigorous will, the servant of a tender conscience; who has learned to love all beauty whether of nature or art, to hate all vileness, and to respect others as himself.[34]

The connection with Spencer is, if anything, even more direct. They met on numerous occasions and commented on and reviewed each other's work. In his Autobiography Bain acknowledged a particular debt to the revised version of Spencer's Principles of Psychology.[35] The relations between the two men appear to have been warm for William L. Davidson remarks that in the closing years of Bain's life 'Herbert Spencer's letters were particularly welcome'.[36] Spencer's collection of articles, Education: Intellectual, Moral and Physical (1861), in which he examined the relative worthwhileness of various kinds of knowledge, had been the subject of considerable debate, and there are good grounds for thinking that many of Bain's educational ideas were derived from this work.

One important qualification is necessary in relation to both Huxley and Spencer. Bain's commitment to the doctrine of evolution was limited. He was certainly fully familiar with Darwinian ideas and their implications for fields other than biology and natural history - indeed he spent a fortnight in Darwin's company at a hydropathic establishment in 1857,[37] during which they discussed the researches on which The Origin of Species was based. Again, the later editions of The Senses and the Intellect and The Emotions and the Will show signs of amendment in the light of the Darwinian revolution. Nonetheless, there is some justice in the observation of one early commentator that 'Bain's psychology is essentially pre-evolutionary',[38] in the sense that the strong presence of older traditions in Bain's thinking - such as those represented by James Mill's Analysis of the Phenomena of the Human Mind[39] and the Scottish Common Sense School of philosophy[40] - prevented a dramatic conversion. In fact, in a correspondence between Bain and Darwin regarding the latter's Expression of the Emotions (1872), Darwin comments, 'as we look at everything from different points of view, it is not likely that we should agree closely'.[41] This suggests an explanation for the enormous popularity of Bain's writings during his lifetime - they contained just the right mixture of traditional wisdom and innovation to be acceptable. It also suggests one reason why they were overtaken relatively quickly.

Given the kind of intellectual background that has been outlined and the method of enquiry that it led to - rigorously logical, empiricist and positivist, highly sceptical of intuitive and spiritual insights - it is possible to anticipate Bain's approach to educational theory. Education is likely to be viewed as an applied science, its practical applications being based on logic and psychology. An explicit statement of this position is to be found in an address entitled 'Metaphysics and Debating Societies', given to the Edinburgh University Philosophical Society in March 1877:

> I deem it quite possible to frame a practical science applicable to the training of the intellect that shall be precise and definite in a very considerable measure. The elements that make up our intellectual furniture can be stated with clearness; the laws of intellectual growth or acquisition are almost the best ascertained generalities of the human mind; even the most complicated studies can be analysed into their components, partly by psychology and partly by the higher logic.[42]

Education as a Science, published two years later, is largely concerned with this very task and it is now necessary to examine it in more detail.

III

It should perhaps be admitted in advance that this is not an immediately attractive prospect. Referring to Bain's writings, L. S. Hearnshaw makes the comment, 'The book on education is particularly long-winded and tedious'.[43] In a similar vein, J. A. Lauwerys contrasts Bain unfavourably with Herbert Spencer, despite their similarity of outlook on the subject of education: 'Bain ... works out ... the theme enunciated by Spencer - though, alas, much less vigorously and in a much duller way'.[44] These are hardly very encouraging judgements, but it has to be conceded that they represent an understandable response to several decidedly unappealing features of the work - in particular, its repetitiveness and its relentless solemnity of tone.

The dullness is explicable, at least in part, by Bain's characteristic mode of proceeding, one which he had evolved quite early in his career; namely, 'exhaustive study of each individual fact, or part of a fact, that could, for the moment, be taken in isolation'.[45] This technique, in fact, amounts to more than a methodology - it helps to determine the substantive conclusions reached. For example, it clearly lies behind Bain's assertion that 'the largest chapter in the Science of Education must be the following out of all the psychological laws that bear directly or indirectly upon the process of mental acquirement'.[46] Psychology is amenable to the approach adopted by Bain and so it inevitably assumes considerable importance in his view of education.

His actual treatment of psychology is one that would entirely commend itself to some present-day learning theorists: for example, although he does not always use the modern terms, there is extensive reference to such ideas as sequence, pacing, anchorage, reinforcement, recall. It seems fair to conclude that Bain would also have been enthusiastic about the prospects opened up by programmed learning - especially the identification of separate units of learning and their presentation in a structured way. Related to this is Bain's conception of knowledge as a commodity, the teacher's duty being to pass on 'a definite amount of knowledge'.[47] This, in turn, assumes a teacher-dominated system, well-suited to mass provision: 'The learner is a learner and not a teacher or discoverer, and has to receive a great deal with mere passive acquiescence'.[48] Despite his radical sympathies, the extent to which Bain's educational thinking merely reflects the dominant economic and social ideologies of his time is apparent here. His occasional use of metaphoric language tends to confirm this. For example, he refers to the exercise of intellectual skills, such as memory, in terms of their physiological 'cost' or 'expense'.[49] Again, he views moral education in terms of the 'management' of sense pleasures and emotions.[50]

His mechanistic approach to human psychology and to the process of learning also affects his view of curriculum. Three points in particular are worth mentioning. First, he is keen to establish the logical distinctiveness of each branch of knowledge and so his curriculum is very firmly subject-based. This leads him, for example, to be very critical of certain approaches to the 'object lesson' because of its inherent temptations to digression and the introduction of contingent matters. Secondly, Bain is obviously very uneasy about subjects which do not seem to possess a highly differentiated, sequential structure; for instance, his remarks on literature and the arts in general reveal a limited understanding of the kind of 'truth' they are concerned with. And thirdly, his chapter on what he calls 'Education Values' - in which he discusses the relative importance of the various subjects competing for a place in the curriculum - is, as we might expect, informed by a strong practical and utilitarian spirit. Here he clearly owes much to Spencer's analysis of the question 'What knowledge is of most worth?'[51] though he is not as extreme or dogmatic as Spencer in establishing a hierarchy.

So far I have been fairly critical of Education as a Science. It is possible, however, to be more charitable towards some aspects of it. J. W. Tibble even ventures to use the word 'refreshing' to describe Bain's 'semantic questioning' in relation to key educational terms and his 'discussion on learning readiness'.[52] Both of these features invite brief comment.

Chapter 4 takes the form of an analysis of 'certain terms and phrases that suspend great issues, and yet are of ambiguous import'.[53] Among the terms referred to by Bain are memory, judgement, imagination, training, culture and discipline. The approach is essentially philosophical and logical, the aim being to establish the various connotations which the terms may have and, in most cases, to strip away any secondary or digressive associations in order to leave a specific, clear denotation. For example, in the case of 'judgement' distinctions are drawn between several senses of the word - 'simple comparison'; 'the power of comprehending'; 'the application of far-reaching knowledge to determine cause and effect'; 'the giving of a sound decision in conflicting circumstances'.[54] Bain's technique here is not unlike that employed by modern rationalist philosophers of education - the systematic examination of usage, the attempt wherever possible to establish limiting criteria, the delineation of an area of apparent conceptual clarity. The result is that his work suffers from some of the same weaknesses as the writings of people like Hirst and Peters; in particular, it is unnecessarily reductionist in character, in the sense that it fails to acknowledge the extent to which key educational concepts resist neat systems of semantic classification, by virtue of their ineliminable value associations and their highly pervasive quality in relation to human experience. Nevertheless, Bain's attempt at definition is an interesting one, given the extreme confusions attaching to key terms in many earlier educational writings - 'nature' perhaps being the most notorious example.[55]

Tibble's approval of Bain's approach to child development is also deserved. Although it is not the most prominent respect in which he anticipates twentieth-century movements, Bain would certainly have had considerable sympathy with the preoccupations and methods of modern developmental psychologists. He remarks that 'Nothing but observation of cases will avail us here',[56] and indicates the range of subjects that merit attention - pre-school activity, the various stages of maturation, the growing capacity for abstract thinking. Related to this, many of his observations about moral and emotional development contain much sound commonsense - and, again, he manages to avoid the extremes of Spencer's position (on 'natural' punishment, for example[57]).

Before passing on to consider Bain's influence as an educational thinker and its implications for the theory of education, it is instructive to note some omissions from Education as a Science.

First, there is no mention of Herbartian psychology. This is explicable in simple chronological terms. The Herbartian revival did not really make itself felt in Britain until the 1890s, though an article by G. F. Stout did appear in Mind in 1888.[58] The possibility that Bain may have influenced the Herbartians will be considered in the next section.

The second omission is, on the face of it, a very surprising one. It is the lack of a properly developed sociological dimension. Given Bain's familiarity with the work of Mill and Comte, and given his advocacy of the social sciences as subjects to be taught in their own right, it might be expected that he would address himself to the sociology of education itself. In fact he does not. He simply makes conventional assumptions about the equation of knowledge and truth and the use of schooling as a means of social selection and control. Why was this the case? The principal reason would appear to be that disciplines need to become established before their practitioners develop that degree of self-consciousness and reflectiveness about their own ideological assumptions upon which a critical sociology depends. So it was not until later - in the writings of Durkheim[59] - that we see the beginnings of a proper sociology of education.

Thirdly, the degree of historical awareness revealed by Bain is disappointing. It is true that there are quite a few references to contemporary writers, including Arnold, and Pestalozzi is mentioned at several points, but there is no sustained treatment of the evolution of educational ideas. That Bain was certainly aware of the tradition of Western Education is apparent from his essay on 'The Art of Study'[60] in which he traces the contributions of Quintilian, Bacon, Milton, Locke, Isaac Watts, and others. Presumably his non-historical treatment in Education as a Science was dictated by a feeling that the application of distinctively scientific methods to education marked such a significant progression that it rendered unnecessary extensive consideration of earlier theories. This again raises the question of the constituent elements which go to make up educational theory. Is an historical dimension indispensable? There are perhaps grounds for thinking that it is, in view of the recurrence of many key questions in the writings of the great educators of the past: in a sense, educational theory, like philosophy, does not make progress.[61] It is not inappropriate at this point to turn to Bain's own place in the history of education and to try to assess his overall contribution.

IV

As a preliminary, it should be noted that Bain's reputation in the field of psychology is firmly established. He is well-represented in the standard histories, both British and American.[62] Hearnshaw identifies three particular features which distinguish Bain from his predecessors: a clear definition of the scope of psychology as a discipline; an attempt to describe the physiological foundations of psychology; and a proper understanding of the requirements of scientific method.[63] Now it has already been noted that psychology, for Bain, forms the major part of Education as a Science. It does not necessarily follow, however, that Bain's standing in the history of psychology automatically ensures him a significant place in the development of educational theory. To determine that will involve a return to the wider considerations touched on at the outset. What can be said at this stage with some certainty is that while Education as a Science enjoyed considerable popularity in the years immediately following publication - the number of reprints, particularly in the United States, testify to that - after the turn of the century the ideas it expressed were fairly quickly superseded by (or, perhaps more accurately, absorbed into) those of other movements, notably pragmatism and Herbartianism. That is not to say that Bain ceased to have any influence at all, simply that his influence became much less direct and correspondingly more difficult to trace (particularly in view of the complexity of some transatlantic exchanges - in the field of mental testing, for example, a topic which will be referred to more fully later in this section). Let me illustrate the nature of the changes that took place a little more precisely.

The immediate success of Bain's Education as a Science is not at all surprising when one considers the developments that were taking place at the time. The 1870 Education Act in England and Wales (1872 in Scotland) had created a system of mass education. This, in turn, had implications for teacher training and for the study of education as a university subject. Chairs of education were established in Edinburgh and St. Andrews in 1876. One very practical result of this expansion and development was the need for suitable text-books for students. Bain's work fitted the bill, if only as a temporary measure until people like S. S. Laurie,[64] first Professor of Education at Edinburgh University, produced suitable books of their own. Thus, for example, in the appendix to a publication entitled Education as a University Subject (1883),[65] which gives examples of early courses in education, it is shown that Laurie made reference to Bain - though, interestingly, under the heading 'The History of Education' rather than what Laurie called 'The Theory or Science of Education'.[66] The author of this publication was David Ross,

Principal of the Church of Scotland College in Glasgow (1877-1899) and a Lecturer in Education at Glasgow University. Ross himself 'gave forty lectures on logic, psychology and ethics as applied to education, taking for special study Locke's Thoughts on Education, Spencer's Education, Moral, Physical and Intellectual (sic) and Bain's Education as a Science'.[67] In England and Wales too, Bain's work enjoyed the status of a prescribed text. The 1895 syllabus of the Teachers Certificate Examination, for example, required third year students to study the life and work of Dr Arnold, Quick's Educational Reformers, Sully's The Teachers Handbook of Psychology and Bain's Education as a Science.[68] It is almost certain that similar evidence regarding the placing of Bain's text on prescribed reading lists for students could be found in the United States.[69]

All this is at a simple practical level. To sketch Bain's influence in the history of ideas is a much more difficult and complex undertaking, and only a few hints can be given here. There is much in Bain's philosophy and psychology that would be compatible with the central tenets of pragmatism, a movement which, through the influence of John Dewey, both in the United States and Britain, had a considerable impact on educational thinking. For example, Bain's insistence that belief is essentially related to action[70] lends support to the stress on activity as an essential ingredient of learning found throughout Dewey's writings.[71] Despite such apparent connections, the founders of pragmatism make relatively few references to Bain and those that do exist are sometimes ambiguous, as M. H. Fisch has shown.[72] At least part of the explanation can be found in a point already noted, namely the qualified approval which Bain gave to Darwin's evolutionary principles. Acceptance of Darwinism was much more enthusiastic among pragmatists, so much so that one commentator, drawing on Fisch's paper, observes that 'Darwin made so effective an impression on the founders of pragmatism that the derivation of the main pragmatic principles from Bain's theory of belief was quite forgotten until Peirce referred to it in 1907'.[73]

A similar pattern of largely unacknowledged assimilation can be seen in relation to more specifically educational movements, most notably Herbartianism. In the United States the original Herbart Club was reorganized in 1895 into the National Herbart Society for the Scientific Study of Teaching. Herbart's The Science of Education had first appeared in 1806 but was not translated into English until 1892.[74] It could be argued that Bain's Education as a Science helped to create the climate in which a revival of interest in Herbart was possible but, again, direct connections are hard to establish.[75] The reforming nature of the American Herbartians, who included Dewey, helps to explain why: they were really seeking a more socially radical psychology and pedagogy than could be found in works such as Bain's. Dewey's position is perhaps a crucial one. Herbert M. Kliebard, referring to the 1980s, says:

> This was the period in Dewey's development when he was beginning to move away from the mere translation of psychological concepts into educational terms and starting to consider the curriculum principles that were later to form the basis of the programme of studies at the Laboratory School at the University of Chicago.[76]

Given this broader approach, allied to the much sounder sociological grasp found in Dewey's writings, it is not entirely surprising that in the early twentieth-century Bain's ideas were overlooked or regarded as unacceptably conservative. Thus, for example, an influential book such as T. Percy Nunn's Education: Its Data and First Principles (1920)[77] has nothing at all to say about Bain.

It would, however, be wrong to write Bain off completely after the turn of the century. After all, this was the period when educational psychology began to take off in a significant way and, indeed, to assume a dominance in the shaping of educational theory which it was to hold until the Second World War. One symptom of this development was the growing strength of the mental testing movement and here an indirect connection with Bain can, without distortion or exaggeration, be established. In The Emotions and the Will Bain discussed the possibility of devising ability and aptitude tests and recommended the application of psychology to problems of training, industry and the armed forces.[78] He also wrote an article for an Aberdeen newspaper proposing 'a means of testing moral or emotional intensity of character'.[79] Interestingly, he envisaged no difficulties regarding the appropriate criteria for such tests but saw simulation on the part of subjects as the main drawback. Of greater significance is the fact that Bain appears to have been connected with most of the major figures in the early development of psychometrics, the international character of which is worth stressing. He knew Francis Galton[80] and also met J. McK. Cattell[81], when the latter was a student at Wundt's laboratory in Leipzig. Cattell was, of course, also Galton's assistant for a period of two years. E. L. Thorndike was a pupil of both Cattell and James, whose knowledge of and respect for Bain's work has already been referred to. Again, A. P. Greenway suggests that the French psychologist Alfred Binet was 'greatly influenced' by Bain[82]: the refinement of Binet's work on intelligence testing was undertaken in the United States by Terman and Merrill. After the First World War the influence of the American mental testing movement in Britain, particularly through Godfrey Thomson, was considerable.[83] The network of associationsis, therefore, quite extensive.

Whether Bain's claim to have anticipated some of these developments redounds to his credit or not depends on the view one takes of the way the study of education was pursued in the first half of this century. It also brings us back to the difficult questions about the nature of educational theory which were introduced at the start of this paper. The impulse towards precision and certainty remains powerful, indeed dominant. Perhaps educationists today would be uneasy about allowing that impulse to lead them, as it led Bain, to define education - for practical purposes - simply as 'the work of the schoolmaster'.[84] But the desire to identify a manageable area of activity, regardless of the distortions and oversimplications it occasions, is still very much in evidence. It lies behind the general acceptance of the view of educational theory as consisting of a number of contributory disciplines. I am inclined to think that this model is more than a product of the expansion of knowledge. To put it rather pejoratively, and perhaps unfairly, it also represents a retreat to the apparent safety of narrow technical expertise - defended, of course, by an appeal to that most disreputable of modern concepts, namely professionalism.

It is a retreat in the sense that it amounts to a refusal to grapple with the immensely difficult value questions which underlie all educational provision. Education, by its very nature, carries presuppositions of a moral, social, political, even metaphysical kind, and a proper study of education involves encountering the most fundamental of human values. To try to conduct educational research without constant reference to those values is, at best, blinkered and, at worst, a complete waste of time. It follows that educational research cannot rest content with purely descriptive or explanatory theories and, in so far as such theories are possible, they must be informed by a wider vision of human beliefs and aspirations. I am saying, in effect, that we need to recapture something in the other set of impulses I described at the start - the impulse towards completeness and experiential validity, the impulse which encourages us to regard educational problems, not as purely technical matters, but as part of a wider system of social, moral and political values. Ironically, a nineteenth century writer such as Huxley, who helped to create the climate of opinion which led to the dominance of the scientific movement in education, had a much firmer grasp of those wider realities than most twentieth-century educational researchers.

To some, inevitably, all this will seem vague humanistic talk. It opens the way, it might be argued, for the sort of impressionistic and subjective writing about the aims of education that has long been discredited. That is certainly a danger. But it should be recognized more widely than it is that to say some aspects of a subject like education are not amenable to scientific analysis is not to say anything derogatory about it - it is simply to acknowledge its diverse and composite character. In short, we need to appreciate the limitations as well as the strengths of the methods initiated by people like Mill and Galton and Bain.

If I have overstated my case, it is because, in the present climate, it is a case that needs overstating. Let me, however, by way of conclusion, attempt to avoid the crude dichotomy of 'rationalism' versus 'humanism' by stressing that recognition of the diverse and composite character of education should never cause us to abandon the search for precision in areas where it is appropriate. There is no simple answer to the question 'Is the study of education an Art or a Science?' for it clearly involves substantial elements of both. I will finish with a quotation which seems to me to strike the right balance: 'The sciences and scientific method will probably always leave unanswered the most interesting questions about man and his place in the world. However, we should be very foolish if we did not take into account what science can tell us'.[85]

REFERENCES

[1] D. J. O'Connor, An Introduction to the Philosophy of Education (Routledge and Kegan Paul, London, 1957), chapter 5. Paul Hirst, 'Educational Theory' in The Study of Education (Routledge and Kegan Paul, London, 1966), ed. J. W. Tibble, pp. 29-58. Further contributions by O'Connor and Hirst to the debate about the nature and scope of educational theory can be found in New Essays in the Philosophy of Education (Routledge and Kegan Paul, London, 1973), ed. Glenn Langford and D. J. O'Connor, pp. 47-75.

[2] These terms were suggested by chapter 6 of William A. Reid's book Thinking about the Curriculum (Routledge and Kegan Paul, London, 1978).

[3] This condensed statement does not convey the immense complexity of the forces at work. Cf. Raymond Williams, Culture and Society 1780-1950 (Penguin, Harmondsworth, 1963).

[4] For a useful discussion of 19th-century arguments about the relative merits of scientific and literary culture, including the contributions of Arnold and Huxley, see Margaret Mathieson, The Preachers of Culture (Allen and Unwin, London, 1975), chapters 1-3.

[5] The collection of papers in Tibble, op. cit., illustrate this approach. It is usually accompanied by what might be called 'the myth of synthesis' - i.e. the assumption that some kind of magical integration will take place in the minds of students subjected to separate courses on educational psychology, sociology, history, philosophy, etc.

[6] Paul Hirst, 'Liberal Education and the Nature of Knowledge' in Knowledge and the Curriculum (Routledge and Kegan Paul, London, 1974), pp. 30-53.

[7] It would be misleading to suggest that 'rationalist' and 'scientific' impulses are identical. Some of the problems are discussed in Reid, op. cit.. A detailed analysis would require an historical account of the relations between a whole series of philosophical concepts, includingrealism, positivism, romanticism, idealism. Cf. Raymond Williams, Keywords: A Vocabulary of Culture and Society (Fontana/Croom Helm, London, 1976).

[8] Again, the precise relation between these two terms invites a detailed study which cannot be attempted here.

[9] Alexander Bain, Education as a Science (Kegan Paul, London, 1879).

[10] For a somewhat fuller account of Bain's career, see Sandy Hobbs and David Cornwell, 'A Psychological Approach to Schoolmastering, 1879', Education in the North, Vol. 16 (1979), pp. 63-69. This article is also of interest in respect of its treatment of Bain's place in the history of educational psychology: cf. section III below.

[11] Alexander Bain, Autobiography (Longmans, Green and Co., London, 1904), p. 81.

[12] Ibid., Appendix.

[13] Ibid., p. 200.

[14] Ibid., p. 246.

[15] Alexander Bain, The Senses and the Intellect (Parker, London, 1855). Second edition 1864. Third edition 1868. Fourth edition 1894.

[16] Alexander Bain, The Emotions and the Will (Parker, London, 1859). Second edition 1865. Third edition 1875. Fourth edition 1899.

[17] See Robert Thomson, The Pelican History of Psychology (Penguin, Harmondsworth, 1968), p. 35.

[18] William James, Principles of Psychology, 2 vols. (Macmillan, London, 1890).

[19] See W. Douglas Simpson (ed.), The Fusion of 1860: A Record of the Centenary Celebrations and a History of the United University of Aberdeen 1860-1960 (Oliver and Boyd, Edinburgh and London, 1963), pp. 175-178.

[20] Alexander Bain, Logic, Part I Deduction, Part II Induction (London, 1870).

[21] See Autobiography, pp. 327-333). Also Robert C. Cross, 'Alexander Bain', Aberdeen University Review, XLIV, I (1971), pp. 1-9.

[22] For example, Wundt wrote on 'Central Innervation and Consciousness' in Vol. I (1876), James on 'The Sentiment of Rationality' in Vol. II (1877), and Galton on 'Statistics of Mental Imagery' in Vol. V (1880). A comprehensive index of the contributors to the first series of Mind (1886-1891) can be found in Vol. XVI (1891).

[23] Autobiography, p. 431. The whole question of Bain's influence on the Continent requires a separate study. Cf. Gabriel Compayré, The History of Pedagogy trans. W. H. Payne (Swan Sonnenschein, Lowrey and Co., London, 1888).

[24] Scottish Universities Commission (H.M.S.O., Edinburgh, 1878), Vol. 2, pp. 667-681.

[25] See Autobiography, pp. 340, 342, 352. Also Hobbs and Cornwell, op. cit., p. 68. Bain's own account of these contributions raises certain problems - e.g., he refers variously to 'the Education Society' and 'the Society for the Development of the Science of Education' - which invite further investigation.

[26] Autobiography, pp. 358-360, 375.

[27] George E. Davie, The Democratic Intellect, 2nd edn. (Edinburgh University Press, 1964), pp. 98-99, 101.

[28] See Cross, op. cit..

[29] The only detailed study I have come across is Ned A. Shearer, 'Alexander Bain and the Classification of Knowledge', Journal of the History of the Behavioral Sciences, Vol. X, No. 1 (1974), pp. 56-73. I am indebted to Professor Eric Forbes of Edinburgh University for drawing my attention to this article.

[30] *Autobiography*, p. 223.

[31] *Ibid.*, p. 153.

[32] *Ibid.*, pp. 156-159.

[33] Herbert Spencer, *Education: Intellectual, Moral, and Physical* (Watts, London, 1949). First published 1861. T. H. Huxley, *Collected Essays*, Vol. III 'Science and Education' (Macmillan, London, 1893).

[34] Huxley, *op. cit.*, p. 86.

[35] *Autobiography*, p. 302.

[36] *Ibid.*, p. 422.

[37] *Ibid.*, pp. 249-250.

[38] Howard C. Warren, *A History of the Association Psychology* (Constable, London, 1921), p. 104.

[39] James Mill, *Analysis of the Phenomena of the Human Mind* (London, 1829).

[40] See Davie, *op. cit.*, Part 4.

[41] *Autobiography*, p. 320.

[42] In *Practical Essays* (Longmans, Green and Co., London, 1884), p. 147.

[43] L. S. Hearnshaw, *A Short History of British Psychology 1840-1940* (Methuen, London, 1964), p. 299.

[44] J. A. Lauwerys, 'Herbert Spencer and the Scientific Movement' in *Pioneers of English Education* (Faber, London, 1952), ed. A. V. Jüdges, p. 188.

[45] *Autobiography*, p. 106.

[46] *Education as a Science*, p. 15.

[47] *Ibid.*, p. 103.

[48] *Ibid.*, p. 95.

[49] *Ibid.*, p. 13.

[50] *Ibid.*, p. 178.

[51] Spencer, *op. cit.*, chapter I.

[52] Tibble, *op. cit.*, p. 8.

[53] *Education as a Science*, p. 120.

[54] *Ibid.*, pp. 122-124.

[55] See C. P. Kimber, 'A Study of the Word 'Nature' in the History of Educational Thought', unpublished M. Ed. thesis (University of Glasgow, 1968).

[56] *Education as a Science*, p. 185.

[57] *Ibid.*, pp. 118-119. Cf. Spencer, *op. cit.*, chapter III.

[58] For a full discussion of the fluctuating reputation of Herbart, see Harold B. Dunkel, *Herbart and Herbartianism: An Educational Ghost Story* (University of Chicago Press, 1970).

[59] See Ivor Morrish, *Disciplines of Education* (Allen and Unwin, London, 1967), chapter 11.

[60] In *Practical Essays*, pp. 201-254.

[61] G. H. Bantock offers an interesting and provocative discussion of the need for historical awareness in educational theory in 'The Parochialism of the

Present: Some Reflections on the History of Educational Theory', Journal of Philosophy of Education, Vol. 13 (1979), pp. 41-54.

62 In addition to the studies of Hearnshaw and Thomson cited above, see J. C. Flugel, A Hundred Years of Psychology (Duckworth, London, 1933); A. A. Roback, History of American Psychology (Library Publishers, New York, 1952); Robert I.,Watson, The Great Psychologists, 3rd edn. (Lippincott, New York, 1971); and Richard J. Herrnstein and Edwin G. Boring (eds), A Source Book in the History of Psychology (Harvard University Press, 1965). For more specialized studies, see two articles by J. A. Cardno: 'Bain and Physiological Psychology', Australian Journal of Psychology, Vol. 7, No. 2 (1955), pp. 108-120; 'Bain as a Social Psycholgist', Australian Journal of Psychology, Vol. 8, No. 1 (1956), pp. 66-76.

63 Hearnshaw, op. cit., p. 2.

64 See Alexander Morgan, Makers of Scottish Education (Longmans, Green and Co., 1929), chapter 13.

65 Extracts from Ross's work are given in Marjorie Cruickshank, A History of the Training of Teachers in Scotland (University of London Press, 1970) pp. 246-250.

66 Ibid., p. 247.

67 Ibid., p. 105.

68 Tibble, op. cit., p. 6.

69 The Herbartian Charles DeGarmo taught a course entitled 'Philosophy of Education' at the University of Illinois during session 1890-91. The University Catalogue reported that 'the basis of this work will be Bain's Education as a Science and Rosenkranz's Philosophy of Education'. I am indebted to Professor Erwin Johanningmeier of the University of South Florida for this information. It seems probable that further evidence could be found at other American Universities.

70 See, for example, The Emotions and the Will, 3rd edition, pp. 505-507.

71 The relation between Dewey and Bain merits further study. It is instructive to compare Bain's Education as a Science with Dewey's The Sources of a Science of Education (Liveright, New York, 1929). Dewey's contributions to Mind in the 1880s provide another line of investigation.

72 Max H. Fisch, 'Alexander Bain and the Genealogy of Pragmatism', Journal of the History of Ideas, Vol. XV, No. 3 (1954), pp. 413-444.

73 A. P. Greenway, 'The Incorporation of Action into Associationism: The Psychology of Alexander Bain', Journal of the History of the Behavioral Sciences, Vol. IX, No. 1 (1973), p. 43. I am indebted to Professor Eric Forbes of Edinburgh University for drawing my attention to this article.

74 J. F. Herbart, The Science of Education trans. H. M. Felkin and E. Felkin (Swan Sonnenschein and Co., London, 1892).

75 Though see note 69 above.

76 Herbart M. Kliebard, 'The Evolution of John Dewey's Theory of Curriculum: The Michigan Period, 1884-1894', paper presented at the University of Bonn, September 1978. I am indebted to Professor Kliebard for permission to quote from his paper prior to publication in the Journal of Curriculum Theorizing.

77 For a discussion of the significance of Nunn's book, see Tibble, op. cit., pp. 11-15.

78 The Emotions and the Will, chapter I.

[79]The Aberdeen Banner (1842). See Autobiography, pp. 131-132.

[80]Autobiography, p. 379.

[81]Ibid., p. 378. See also p. 391. Cattell published an article entitled 'Mental Tests and Measurements' in Mind, Vol. XV (1890), pp. 373-381.

[82]Greenway, op. cit., p. 49.

[83]For detailed discussions of Thomson's influence, see H. M. Paterson, 'Godfrey Thomson and the Development of Psychometrics in Scotland', and R. E. Bell, 'Godfrey Thomson and Scottish Education'. Both papers were presented at the British Educational Research Association Conference in 1975 and abbreviated versions can be found in Research Intelligence, B E R A Bulletin 2 (1975), pp. 63-68.

[84]Autobiography, p. 342.

[85]Patricia Smart, 'Education: An Art or a Science?', Proceedings of the Philosophy of Education Society of Great Britain, Vol. VIII, No. 1 (1974), p. 75.

JOHANN FRIEDRICH HERBART : HIS CONTRIBUTION TO EDUCATIONAL THOUGHT AND PRACTICE

J. W. L. Adams
Professor, Department of Education
University of Dundee

ABSTRACT

As an academic philosopher Herbart must have had an intellectual history. Yet important aspects of this development remain obscure. From the vantage point of education, the key question concerns the relationship between the psychology (upon which many of his educational recommendations were based) and the overall philosophical system. A crucially important consideration here appears to have been the pressure on Herbart (in common with other aspiring philosophers in German universities) to produce a fully-fledged system of metaphysics in order to further his academic career. For the sake of completeness, Herbart's philosophic system is outlined and discussed in this paper under the following heads:

(1) The need for metaphysics
(2) Psychology
(3) Presentation and apperception
(4) The 'nature/nurture' controversy
(5) 'Morality : the Sole and Total Task of Education'
(6) The self
(7) 'Instruction builds the circle of thought; education the character'.

The available evidence, however, suggests that the origins of the Herbartian philosophy can most convincingly be located in Herbart's own classroom and tutoring experiences. The line of development, therefore, (contrary to Herbart's own assertions) would run from pedagogy via psychology to the grand philosophy. Retention of the salient features of the psychology and ethics by later Herbartians, as well as their neglect of the philosophic system as a whole, would then be readily comprehensible.

Although Herbart aimed to develop a rigorously mathematical psychology, his approach was highly idiosyncratic and bore little apparent resemblance to the statistical approaches of later experimental psychologists. From the point of view of the present conference theme, he is therefore perhaps best viewed as a collateral rather than a direct ancestor of 'The Scientific Movement in Educational Research'.

****

First, I should like to congratulate the organizers of this conference for the theme they have chosen, 'The Scientific Movement in Educational Research'. I take it that this is a deliberate incursion by the Scottish History of Education Society into the most important kind of history, but also the most difficult, the history of ideas. I think I know how tricky the undertaking is, for I was first introduced to these matters at Oxford by that great man H. M. Last, probably the best all-round scholar of my time.

The subject is well worth investigation. One of the most eminent people in this field at the moment is Sir Isaiah Berlin, first president of Wolfson College, Oxford, President of the British Academy, and Fellow of All Souls. Let me set the background for my remarks by quoting a passage, written by Roger Hausheer, from the Introduction to Berlin's recently-published collection of essays, Against the Current (Hogarth Press, 1979, p. xvil).

> There is a growing feeling that investigation of what men have thought and felt, and of the basic ideas in terms of which they have seen themselves and framed their aspirations, may provide a more luminous source of light in the study of man than the established social, political, and psychological sciences, for all that many of these have developed an apparatus of specialised terminology and the use of empirical, quantitative methods. For in so far as they tend to view men, both as individuals and groups, as the proper objects of the generalising empirical sciences, as so much passive, inexpressive material moulded by impersonal forces obedient to statistical or causal laws, these scientists tend to leave out, or at least play down, something of central importance: namely that men are defined precisely by their possession of an inner life, of purposes and ideals, and of a vision or conception, however hazy or implicit, of who they are, where they have come from, and what they are at. And indeed, it is just their possession of an inner life in this sense that distinguishes them from animals and natural objects.

(To anticipate, there is much in this passage with which Herbart would have agreed. He seems to have held, for example, that there could be no experimental psychology because there is no such thing as mind in general, each mind is unique, and that is that. Of course, he was inconsistent in this.)

Perhaps this passage may also serve as a reason (an excuse?) for my own presence at a gathering examining 'the scientific movement in educational research', a movement in which I have had no part. Otherwise, you might well be saying, with the Book of Samuel: 'And it came to pass, when all that knew him beforetime saw that, behold, he prophesied among the prophets, then the people said one to another, What is this that is come unto the son of Kish? Is Saul also among the prophets?' Or, if you prefer Moliere to the Bible - 'Mais que diable allait-il faire dans cette galère?'

But to Herbart. 'Johann Friedrich Herbart', says Adams (the other one) 'was born in 1776, and died in 1841'. So far so good. But he goes on 'He has no history. Philosophers seldom have. It is a compensation'. (The Herbartian Psychology, p. 45.) What nonsense! 'Philosophers seldom have a history' - forsooth! Who will be our examples? Locke was up to the neck in the plottings against James VII, and had to seek refuge in Holland; Hegel had an illegitimate son, by a lady, Christiana Burkhardt (nee Fischer), who already had two children, born, as the records say, 'in dishonour'. Nietzsche (perhaps he doesn't count?) had a tortured life and finally became insane; Descartes was almost literally killed by Queen Christina; Bertrand Russell tells us that he often, when young, contemplated suicide, and so on. But perhaps Adams means 'no intellectual history'? The answer is - if he was a philosopher, he must have had an intellectual history, a development. Philosophers, unlike Minerva, their patroness, don't spring fully-armed from the head of their father. Indeed, in his later years, Gilbert Ryle spent a lot of time arguing (rightly) that Plato must have had a development and trying to trace it. The fact that the resultant book, Plato's Progress, was not very well received by scholars is beside the point. Nobody argued that Plato didn't have a progress: they simply disagreed with Ryle's suggested outline of it. In fact, Professor Harold B. Dunkel in his recent book Herbart and Herbartianism: an Educational Ghost Story (University of Chicago Press, 1970) - to which I am much indebted, as are we all - tells us quite a lot about Herbart's 'history'. He was badly burned as a child by falling 'into a kettle' of boiling water (a considerable feat, one would think), and he had a dreadfully over-protective mother, who went with him to the university, debating societies, and so on, and hobnobbed with his teachers, notably Fichte. But neither in Dunkel's book, nor in the only other adequate treatment of Herbart in modern times that is known to me, C. D. Hardie's Truth and Fallacy in Educational Theory (Cambridge University Press, 1942) can I find a satisfactory answer regarding the details of Herbart's intellectual history. (But Dunkel, I think, does indicate the direction in which we should look.) In particular, I can't find an answer to the all-important question, from an educational point of view, which is, roughly, this: - Given that Herbart figures quite prominently in histories of educational thought, and that his theories, particularly his psychological theories, were at one time expounded in training colleges and universities, and given that Herbart himself always insisted that his whole philosophy was 'all of a piece', and that no one bit of it could be properly understood without the rest, given all this, which came first, the hen or the egg? Or, in other words, did the whole massive edifice arise from his psychology (which everybody seems to agree was reasonably applicable in the classroom), or did the psychology (which Herbart always insisted derived from his metaphysics) just happen to have classroom application? As I say, I don't know the answer. But perhaps I can 'beat about the neighbouring fields', as Hume said, or perhaps 'the neighbouring bushes'.

I cannot claim to be, in any way, an 'expert' on Herbart, and indeed I have not read any of his books in the original German. On the other hand, I doubt if I would lose much money if I offered £1 to any member of this audience who had. (No prizes for those who claim to have read the chapter on Herbart in R. R. Rusk's The Doctrines of the Great Educators. Dr Rusk has the (to me) disconcerting habit of jumping about, almost like a flea, all over the Herbartian corpus, and I find it very difficult to extract a clear and coherent picture. I have heard rumours that someone is bringing out a new edition of Rusk. One will see what is made of Herbart, but one has one's forebodings.) But to return. No doubt some of us should set to and plough through all Herbart, but, as his far greater contemporary, Goethe, said:

> Ach Gott, die Kunst ist lang,
> Und kurz ist unser Leben.

Ars longa, vita brevis. And when I read German, it is much more likely to be Goethe. The great Porson is reputed to have said that life is too short to learn German. Had Herbart lived fifty years earlier, he might have written in Latin; and Porson would have had no grouse. I once put all Pestalozzi into our class library, and, to give me my due, I have always meant to do the same for Herbart.

I am not really wandering from my theme, for one of the things which emerges very clearly from Dunkel's valuable book is the great gulf that lies fixed between Herbart and the Herbartians. Hence his additional title - 'An Educational Ghost Story'. It would appear that 'the Herbartians', especially those who were not Germans, did not bother too much either about the original philosophy of the Master. In a recently-published symposium on Nietzsche (Studies in Nietzsche and the

Classical Tradition, edited by James C. O'Flaherty, Timothy F. Sellner, and Robert M. Helm; University of North Carolina Press, 1976), Professor Hugh Lloyd-Jones, Regius Professor of Greek at Oxford, informs us that Nietzsche said 'Only a genius can write clearly in German'. To judge from Dunkel's report, by this yard-stick, Herbart was not a genius. Philosophically, he was a contemporary of, and a rival to, people who were certainly in the Premier League - Kant, Hegel, Fichte, Schelling, Schiller. To us, poor Anglophones, they are all very difficult - I am tempted to say, needlessly difficult. Kant has been described (by Russell, I think) as having contrived to be 'technical without being precise'. Sir Malcolm Knox has recently defended Hegel as a stylist in German Life and Letters and Sir Malcolm certainly knows what he is talking about, but to me it is not convincing. He stresses such well-known remarks of Hegel as the one about the Owl of Minerva only taking to flight when the shades of night are falling, but goes on to admit that even he (Knox) has difficulty, on occasion, in seeing, in a complex sentence, how the relative pronouns fit in. One wise-crack hardly makes a stylist. Last session, for an M.Ed. special paper on aesthetic education, I thought of prescribing Schiller On the Äesthetic Education of Man (Uber die Asthetische Erziehung des Menschen) but, despite the admirable edition and translation by Wilkinson and Willoughby (Clarendon Press, 1967), I thought better of it. It was in this league that Herbart was competing, a league where it seemed to be required that a professor of philosophy should perform in an amazingly complicated and involved style. And, according to Dunkel, he performed accordingly. Porson wasn't so far wrong, after all.

The next point is that this German Premier League ('Bundesliga'?) was composed of metaphysicians, system-builders. When I was young at Oxford, and a Logical Positivist (Ayer was just back from Vienna) metaphysics ('l'art de s'egarer avec methode') was a dirty word, and Hegel the prime target. (I remember explaining all this to Professor McClelland, who found it rather congenial, but amazing, he thought, coming from someone of my background.) We thought we had done with metaphysics (and theology) once and for all. And that was a relief. If you try to read a bit of Herbart, on his 'Reals', say, or on what he calls 'Eidolology' (the possibility of knowledge and its limits) - in an English translation, of course, you will soon see what I mean. You might even, like Hermann Goering, reach for your revolver. But then, but then ... Metaphysics, like Nature in Horace, came back: 'usque recurret'. A moderately careful reading of Wittgenstein's Tractatus will show that it is metaphysics, and that he is telling us that it is metaphysics. Metaphysics isn't dead (ask Strawson), nor is theology. (Here I am tempted to say, 'alas'). But nobody nowadays writes the kind of metaphysics that Herbart wrote. He was a man of his time. How could we expect him, and him alone, to resist the 'Weltgeist'? An aspiring German academic had to produce his own system. Dunkel shows that, by the time he was in his early thirties, at Göttingen, he had, as the saying went, 'found his system', and could look for due promotion in the German academic hierarchy. (To me, it seems a rather grim and humourless world. And surely an educational system was mad that started boys on philosophy at 12, as Herbart did.) At Koenigsberg he succeeded Kant, the greatest of them all, though not immediately, as some books state, or imply.

What was his system? I suppose I must make some attempt to expound it, for to some extent the argument depends on at least some vague outline. But I ought to begin by saying that nowadays, in this country at least, Herbart the philosopher is ignored. There is an article on him in The Encyclopedia of Philosophy (by Harold B. Dunkel!), and he is given about four pages in Emile Bréhier's Histoire de la Philosophie. But he is not mentioned in Russell's History of Western Philosophy or in the Critical History of Western Philosophy, edited by D. J. O'Connor, or in Antony Flew's Introduction to Western Philosophy, or in Western Philosophy and Philosophers, edited by J. O. Urmson. But, to be fair, let me quote the concluding paragraph from the article on Herbart by Ward, in the

the eleventh edition of the Encyclopedia Britannica (1910-1911). It will at least remind us of the extra-ordinary change of fashion that has taken place in philosophy, and to which I have already referred:

> Among the post-Kantian philosophers Herbart doubtless ranks next to Hegel in importance, and this without taking into account his very great contribution to the science of education. His disciples speak of theirs as the 'exact philosophy', and the term well expresses their master's chief excellence and the character of the chief influence he has exerted upon succeeding thinkers of his own and other schools. His criticisms are worth more than his constructions; indeed for exactness and penetration of thought he is quite on a level with Hume and Kant. His merits in this respect, however, can only be appraised by the study of his works at first hand. But we are most of all indebted to Herbart for the enormous advance psychology has been enabled to make, thanks to his fruitful treatment of it, albeit as yet but few among the many who have appropriated and improved his materials have ventured to adopt his metaphysical and mathematical foundations.

The system then. What distinguishes philosophy from other activities according to Herbart is not its subject matter, but its method. It reworks concepts to make them clear and distinct, and to remove contradictions. The fundamental move seems to be that we keep coming up against cases where we are tempted to assert that S is both P and not-P, which is logically intolerable. This seems to be a form of the application of the age-old so-called Law of the Excluded Middle. Herbart was trained, and gifted, in music, and it has been suggested that, at the back of the philosopher's mind, was an analogy concerning the compatibility and incompatibility of notes - harmonies and discords. Or again (pace Adams) that it was from the troubles of his own early life that he derived this emphasis on harmony and the avoidance of contradiction. The process of Herbart's analysis results in the conclusion that there are three main branches of philosophy:- logic, metaphysics (from which psychology is derived), and aesthetics (under which comes ethics). Ethics gives the aims of education, and psychology its methods. The reason for metaphysics is this: (Dunkel) 'experience gives rise to many concepts which, the more distinct they become, the more contradictory they appear ... Our ideas must, therefore, undergo an 'enlargement' (Ergänzung), which will remove the contradiction'. The third branch (aesthetics), arises because, in this area, we find not only a need for enlargement: we find that there is also involved 'an intuitive judgment of approval or disapproval'.

So much, however inadequate, by way of outline. Perhaps I may offer a few comments:

1. The need for metaphysics. The problem is 'What changes?', which is perhaps the perfect, all-embracing, metaphysical question. 'To distinguish between that which is, and has no becoming, and that which always becomes but never is.' Herbart seems to have been worried about this question - those of you who havenot been bitten by the philosophical bug may well say that this is the kind of question that only a philosopher would worry about. One of the causes of this worry was the old Greek philosopher, Parmenides, whose fragments (they are all we have) were collected and published when Herbart was a student. It has been said that ever since Parmenides, who denied the possibility of change, the philosophical world has never been quite sane. Herbart's answer, not unlike Kant's, was that we have to 'posit' (a favourite word with metaphysicians in Herbart's time) a world of 'reals', which underlie, in some way, the world of appearances, which reveals itself to our senses.

2. Psychology. One of these 'reals' is the human soul. But it is an 'ensouled' real. This apparently satisfied the Lutheran church authorities. The soul was preserved, and hence Christian doctrines about its immortality and so on were not impugned. Dunkel says:

> The conjunction and the separation of the reals explain these sensible appearances which led to their postulation. Such mutual interaction would seem to lead to mutual destruction, but, just as in an equilibrium of forces both forces remain constantly what each is, though balanced, so in the concatenation of reals, the mutual perturbations (Störungen) which would lead to mutual destruction are counterbalanced by individual acts of self-preservation through which each real strives to remain what it is.

'Everything in mind arises in some form out of presentations. There are no faculties, no innate ideas, no concepts a priori.' This denial of faculties seems to have been welcomed, in due course, by educational psychologists, who seem to have derived comfort from it in their campaign against 'traditional' subjects like Latin and Greek. 'The soul is a real in which countless acts of self-preservation are provoked through its contacts with other reals.' The reals and presentations can apparently 'be understood by analogy with forces' (Dunkel), and in this way Herbart, the mathematician, was able to offer a kind of statics and mechanics of mind. Ward's article in the eleventh edition of the Encyclopedia Britannica will perhaps help to give a sample of the equations which Herbart produced on this basis, equations which quantify the relations of apperceptive masses, and so on.

The important point for us is that it is here that Herbart applied mathematics to psychology. It seems to me to be a far cry from the statistical prodedures which are presumably the theme of this conference. Other members of the conference will probably enlighten me, but at present I am not at all clear that Herbart, on this score, could be considered a direct ancestor of the 'scientific movement in educational research'.

Perhaps another point should be made, which, if valid, would make us doubt Herbart's procedure. He seems to have thought that in 'positing' the elements of his equations (he admitted that they were 'fictions') he was doing the same thing as, and following in the steps of, Newton. But the Newtonian 'fictions' have a practical, pragmatic function: they can be used for prediction, and can send men to the moon and pieces of machinery to Saturn, and so on. The Herbartian 'fictions' seem to have no future, despite what Ward said, no application, no predictive power. They may have an explanatory power; I wouldn't know, but it might be a point for discussion. I cannot resist adding that, if Herbart's equations do have an explanatory power, as Ward would seem to hold, but not a predictive power, the situation would remind me of the contrast that I seem to find between the remarks made by 'pure' scientists and those of social scientists. 'Pure' scientists are quite willing to predict: social scientists generally are not. Is this because many of the social scientists have not yet found their Newton? Newton? Have they even found their Copernicus? Or, to be honest, even their Ptolemy? Or am I being provocative?

3. Presentation and Apperception. It seems to me that Herbart's explanation of what goes on 'in the mind' (perhaps more of a metaphor than he would admit) is curiously satisfying, despite the mathematics, and corresponds reasonably well with what we find when we introspect. Even the bit about 'arching' and 'vaulting' and being pulled up into consciousness (Wölbung and Hebung and so on) makes some kind of sense, when one thinks about it. And this seems to be the part of Herbart that appealed to those who applied the system to education - if one may judge from

Adams' The Herbartian Psychology applied to Education. Adams' book is a curious production, and now seems very dated. It is written in an oddly condescending and 'arch' style, and does not seem to assume any great learning (or even ability) on the part of its readers; in other words, for 'elementary' teachers. But one can see how the 'Five Steps' (Vorbereitung, Darbietung, Verknüpfung, Zusammenfassung, Anwendung) which Herbart's original Four Steps had become, attracted later pedagogues, and became an ideal frame-work for 'crit' lessons. It is not so long since they disappeared from the scene, to judge from the reports of our Diploma classes, if indeed they have disappeared. Herbart's theory also offered an explanation of individual differences, but I doubt if there is time to deal with that. I am reminded of the Wordsworthian pastiche:

A violet by a mossy stone
A yellow primrose was to him
But O, the difference to me.

4. The 'Nature/Nurture' controversy. Herbart was undoubtedly ingenious, and one is bound to admire his way of getting round this problem. (Here I am much indebted to Hardie.) What lets Herbart out of the dilemma is, of course, the 'soul' which he 'posits'. This enables him to argue that, as Hardie puts it, 'mind is reducible to matter plus a certain factor (soul) which is qualitatively the same in all'. Hence 'variations in mind are due to variations either in the original bodily state (nature) or in the environment (nurture), or in both'. Whatever you may think of this argument, it opens the way for Herbart's next move, which is to argue that, since variations in the bodily state cannot be controlled, education must concentrate on variations on the environment, hence instruction is all-important, and hence Herbart's celebrated dictum 'I confess to have no conception of education without instruction'.

5. 'Morality: the Sole and Total Task of Education'. Herbart goes on, 'Just as, on the other hand, I recognise no instruction which does not morally educate'. For my part, I find Herbart's treatment of morality curiously satisfactory, more satisfactory, indeed than the neo-Kantianism which seems to be at present in vogue, because of the influence of Hare. This for two or three reasons:

(a) As we have seen, Herbart subsumes ethics under aesthetics. This rings a sympathetic bell in me. I suspect that the ancient Greeks would have agreed too. Their language shows it. 'Kalos' is a word that can be used for both moral and aesthetic appraisal, and even 'hamartia' has performative/aesthetic overtones. It hardly means 'sin'. I think it was J. L. Mencken who said that 'Sin is a Jewish invention'. When I come across an action of which I disapprove morally, I find that I tend to classify it as not 'kalon', i.e. 'ugly', unbefitting the style of a creature who has some claims to a relationship with 'beauty'.

(b) Herbart's treatment of moral judgments and moral disagreements is also very plausible. He claims that a right action will show certain characteristics. (It would seem that these do not amount to a definition, but some of them are always present when we use the word 'right'.) He then outlines these five marks. They are:

(i) 'Inner Freedom' - an agreement between the action and my judgment of it.
(ii) 'Perfection of Will' - 'the stronger and more concentrated will is superior to the weaker'. These two characteristics can be observed by the person who wills : the next three are open to public observation. They are:
(iii) 'Benevolence'
(iv) 'Justice'
(v) 'Equity'. These three have their usual meaning.

Now comes the attractive part of the argument. If two people disagree about how to characterize an action, they go over these points. If they agree about them but still disagree about whether the action is right or wrong, all they can do is to separate, on the assumption that they are speaking different moral languages. The situation (this is Hardie's example) is just as if what I call a dog, you call a rabbit.

(c) I also find Herbart's argument about the central position of morality in education at least as satisfying as that of Peters and his disciples. But anyway they tend in the same direction.

6. The Self. Even his description of the apperception-masses, and their relationship to the Self, is very plausible. To quote Ward:

> Self-consciousness is the result of an interaction essentially the same in kind as that which takes place when a comparatively simple presentation finds the fields of consciousness occupied by a long-formed and well consolidated 'mass' of presentations - as, e.g. one's business or garden, the theatre, etc., which promptly inhibit the isolated presentation if incongruent, and unite it to themselves if not. What we call Self is, above all, such a central mass, and Herbart seeks to show with great ingenuity and detail how this position is occupied at first chiefly by the body, then by the seat of ideas and desires, and finally by that first-personal Self which recollects the past and resolves concerning the future.

7. 'Instruction builds the circle of thought; education the character'. The 'circle of thought' notion seems to be Herbart's anticipation of Hirst's writings on a Liberal Education. To me, Herbart makes more sense than Hirst's stress on the internal 'logic' of various forms of mental activity, and Hirst is not a great advance on Aristotle. Aristotle, of course, is not mentioned by Hirst.

So much by way of comment. Now we come to the 'ghost story'.

Herbart could hardly have foreseen his 'Nachleben' - which of us can? He was perhaps a bit disappointed when he returned from Koenigsberg to Göttingen (and, after he died, his wife, who was English, quickly returned to East Prussia). The Prussian government seems to have had doubts about his pedagogical activities, and perhaps felt that his 'demonstration school' was too individualist, and not closely enough in touch with the 'Gymnasium'. After all, by the 1840s the Gymnasia of Humboldt were presumably in full swing. (I wish, incidentally, that someone would tell us of the school of Schulpforta, which, just about the time of Herbart's death, was producing an amazing string of pupils, including both Nietzsche and Wilamowitz-Moellendorf.) As I said before, Herbart did not leave a 'school' in the way the other 'masters' did, not only in philosophy, but in every conceivable academic subject. It was the age which is described in Lord Acton's essay 'German Schools of History', in the first volume of the English Historical Review in 1886. But one or two people who could be called Herbartians lived on. In particular Ziller taught at Leipsig, and Rein and Stoy at Jena. They are the thread which stretches across the period from 1841 to the 60s and 70s. Dunkel has a chapter entitled 'Ziller transforms the Labyrinth', and the next one is called 'Rein makes the Doctrine useful'. A drastic process of excision took place, and as a result the Herbartian metaphysics sank, almost without trace. The notion that the curriculum should somehow recapitulate the history of the human race became prominent. Herbart himself had looked kindly on the recapitulation idea, and had used the Odyssey with

with the Swiss boys he had tutored, because it represents the 'boyhood' of Greece, and hence, presumably, of western civilisation. (The theory had a long run. In 1937, at Dundee Training College, I was awarded an Educational Institute of Scotland Prize for an essay on the theme (set by Professor McClelland) 'The Mental Characteristics of Adolescence and their Implications for the Teaching of the Classics'. I can't lay my hands on it now, but I'm sure it was on good Herbartian lines.) Ziller was, however, much more interested than Herbart had been in the development of elementary schools, as was natural, when we think of the social and economic development that must have taken place in a Germany which had seen unification and the rise of Bismarck. The Odyssey gave way to the Old Testament worthies, and even to Grimm's Fairy Tales, and (thanks to Rousseau) to Robinson Crusoe. The Herbartian psychology was expressed in various schemes whereby the 'circle of thought' could keep on expanding, through annual 'concentration centres'.

But, if the metaphysics disappeared, the psychology and ethics remained in some form. In particular, I think, the stress on many-sided interest and apperception. Here is another of Herbart's notions with which I have much sympathy. Roughly, the argument is as follows (again, I largely follow Hardie): a good individual is one who habitually wills rightly. What this means has been 'explicated', as they say nowadays, by the five Moral Ideas. Our acts of will are determined by our desires, when the objects of these desires seem attainable. Our desires are determined by our interests, and our interests are determined by instruction. In this system, the role of the teacher was obviously central, and one can see how it fitted into a society where schools and training colleges were multiplying.

This was the situation when the first American educationists went to Germany, De Garmo and the McMurry brothers, in the 1880s. The nineteenth century was the German century. In the middle of the century the German states had scores of universities, with each department pursuing its appropriate Wissenschaft, whereas in England Oxford and Cambridge still awaited reform, and outside them there were only the stripling London and Durham. (Scotland was another story, of course.) But no wonder the Americans flocked to Germany for higher degrees. So did we. I myself was taught science at Arbroath High School by a Scot with a German doctorate. Rhodes had not yet created his foundation, and it was only after the Kaiser War that Britain tried to move, deliberately, into the market for aspiring American Ph Ds.

So Herbart and Herbartianism were brought to America, and in the 1890s it became all the rage. A Herbartian society was founded, but it lasted only five or six years as 'Herbartian'. My impression (and I am very much open to correction) is that it was absorbed in wider movements, the growth of sociology, pragmatism, Darwinism and evolutionary biology, and later 'psychometry'. I think that Herbartianism was too individual and too idiosyncratic to be readily absorbed into the twentieth century amalgam. It had perhaps too many technical terms that were not easily translated into other, less specialized, terminologies. 'The mounting popularity of experimental work', says Dunkel, 'was a major threat to Herbartianism and caused some bad blood between the two schools of thought'. My impression is that the British Herbartians were strongly influenced by the Americans. By the time of the Kaiser War the movement was in decline in Britain too. When I sat under McClelland I do not recall that Herbart was ever mentioned. It was all Dewey and Schiller (again, the other one!). And of course Percy Nunn, whose individualism I see as a reaction against the Kaiser's Germany, and as the educational analogue to The Metaphysical Theory of the State, by L. T. Hobhouse. Both books appeared just at the end of the War.

The syncretism to which I have referred is apparent in the concluding paragraph of Adams' The Herbartian Psychology; 'It is probably too much to say', writes Adams, 'that the Herbartians as a body agree with Dr Harris (W. T.) and Professor

Dewey, but in the meantime it cannot be denied that the latest word of the Herbartians deposes interest from its place as the first principle of education, and makes it rank second to the principle of self-realization'. This seems to me to pull out a central block in the building, and the whole edifice falls down. It is almost as if one were to say 'the latest word of the Christians deposes Jesus from His place'. Adams goes on: 'This outcome of his work would no doubt have greatly surprised J. F. Herbart'. No doubt! 'But if we have drifted somewhat from Herbart, we have drawn nearer to Froebel. That the two opposing systems should tend to meet on common ground is no more than one acquainted with the movement of the Hegelian dialectic would expect'. How bland! And how far away now it all seems. Like the story of the man who proposed to stand as M. P. for Oxford University as a Liberal-Unionist, and 'catch the Hegelian vote'.

Dunkel's first chapter is entitled 'Up like the rocket; down like the stick', and I suppose that adequately described Herbart's 'Nachleben'. As I have indicated, there is much worth preserving, worth remembering, in what he wrote, but it is difficult to incorporate the good points into another system. I do not think he can be considered as a serious ancestor of 'the scientific movement in educational research', but whether that is a point in his favour or not is another matter. Dunkel himself says that 'Herbartian psychology did not easily lend itself to the experimental manipulation which Thorndike, Judd, and the like were making popular'. In the line of descent, he seems to me more like Neanderthal Man - a collateral. I hope my analogy is correct.

In answer to my earlier question, I <u>suspect</u> that his system has its original foundation in his experience in the classroom, or at least with the boys he was tutoring. After all, amongst his earliest works were his comments on Pestalozzi. So the development, despite Herbart's own assertions, would be pedagogy → psychology → his general philosophy. And the Herbartians can be forgiven for discarding the metaphysics.

To me there is much that is attractive in him. Often, he seems to have come quite near to getting the right answers by doing the wrong sums. And, to adapt and modify W. C. Fields' remark about the man who disliked dogs and children, a man cannot be wholly bad who wants pupils to have the opportunity to hear (in the original, of course) 'the surge and thunder of the <u>Odyssey</u>'.

FOOTNOTE

I have tried to incorporate into the text the kind of material that usually figures in footnotes, since I find the modern practice of collecting 'footnotes' on a different page, at the end of a chapter or book, quite detestable. Nor have I offered a bibliography. Those who are interested will find an adequate one in Dunkel's book. Since writing this chapter, I have had the opportunity to read, with profit, the following articles:

'The Evolution of John Dewey's Theory of Curriculum : the Michigan Period, 1884 - 1894', by Herbert M. Kliebard, University of Wisconsin, Madison: presented to a seminar at the University of Bonn, 4-8 September, 1978.

'Ruminations on the Beginnings of Educational Psychology: William James and the Foundations of a Profession', by Erwin V. Johanningmeier, in <u>Educational Theory</u>, 28, No. 2 (Spring, 1978), pp. 111-119.

'Herbartian Repetition in Cognitive Psychology', by Shelley Phillips, in <u>Education for Development</u>, Journal of the Faculty of Education, University College, Cardiff, Vol. 5, No. 2, October, 1978, pp. 39-47.

AMERICAN EDUCATIONAL RESEARCH: APPLICATIONS AND MISAPPLICATIONS OF PSYCHOLOGY TO EDUCATION

Erwin V. Johanningmeier
Research Director, Division of Sponsored Research
University of South Florida

ABSTRACT

Through a consideration of the work of Edward L. Thorndike, Arnold Gesell, Daniel Starch and William C. Bagley, this paper attempts to demonstrate the all-pervasive character of the scientific movement in American education.

****

American educational research, like many things American, is a story of many liaisons and many mixed marriages. Some developments issued from enthusiasm; others for the sake of convenience; and still others out of necessity. It acquired its chief characteristics during the period in which the United States was virtually completing its transformation from an agrarian society of small towns to an industrialized society with large urban and even metropolitan areas. The scale and the character of the public schools, especially the secondary schools, were dramatically changed during this period. As the cities increased their numbers and housed a more diverse population, provided more services, and called for more tax dollars, a steadily increasing percentage of the school-aged youth was attending school, the school term was lengthened and attendance became more regular. The percentage of school-age youth (from five to seventeen years) attending school rose from fifty-seven in 1870 to seventy-eight in 1920. In 1870 there were 6,792,000 pupils enrolled in nursery, kindergarten and grades 1 to 9, and 19,378,000 in 1920. The expansion at the secondary level was even more marked. By 1890 the public high school was the most commonly attended secondary school.

While educators had to contend with the problems associated with the growth of the schools, they also had to contend with those who demanded that the schools serve as a vehicle for social reform. Lawrence A. Cremin has shown that 'proponents of virtually every progressive cause from the 1890s through World War I had their program for the school'.[1] Some were attacking big business and political corruption and the relationship between the two. Some blamed the schools for creating society's ills and others wanted the schools to remedy them.

While American educational researchers were finding a place for themselves in the American university and beginning to fashion their methodologies, a revolution in

American secondary education was occurring. 'The heart of this revolution was', Cremin has noted, 'a shift in the conception of the school, or what could and should be its primary goals and responsibilities'.[2] The contrast between two NEA reports, The Report of the Committee of Ten (1893) and the Report of the Commission on the Reorganization of Secondary Education (1918), illustrates the changes that had occurred. The Committee of Ten conceived of a school for the few; the Commission conceived of a school for all. The Commission saw the high school not as an adjunct to the college but as a 'pivotal point in the public school system, one which carried forward objectives yet unfinished by the elementary school and opened new vistas leading on to the colleges'.[3] From an institution concerned primarily with the cultivation of the intellect, the high school became a vehicle for 'progressive amelioration of every individual and social need'.[4]

As educators debated about the propriety of assigning new purposes and introducing new methods into the public schools, they turned to educational research, especially psychology, to support either their opposition or their endorsements. Professional educators and the public were convincing themselves that science would soon solve their social and educational problems. Those who were trying to investigate educational problems scientifically either became partisans or saw others use the conclusions of their inquiries for partisan purposes. Questions about how children learn and questions about what should be taught and to whom became interwoven and confused one for the other. The many psychological discussions and the many editorial discussions about transfer of training in the first decades of the twentieth century illustrate that Americans wanted to use 'scientific facts' to resolve what were essentially questions of value. In the United States educational researchers were from their very beginnings expected to answer not only questions about what is but also questions about what ought to be. Disinterested, dispassionate inquiry was not common. Educational science was shaped by the social concerns and the social visions of the day.

As the popularity of the high school grew, so did the interest of the universities in developing pedagogy and the 'science of education'. The development of education as a department, study, discipline, or whatever on the university campuses created a demand for qualified professors of the new subject. In some instances, school superintendents or experienced teachers from the normal schools were recruited to fill the new stations. However, the pressures from other quarters of the university called for a faculty that had been properly trained and a faculty that could carry on in the tradition of the graduate school - an institution that Americans were just then establishing.[5] Those who were trying to establish a place for education on the university campus, frequently did so by arguing that their work was related to or very much like that of psychology, a discipline that had only recently established its independence from philosophy. However, the separation of psychology from philosophy was then far from complete.

While some philosophers turned to psychology, some psychologists still carried philosophical baggage. Educators frequently employed both psychology and philosophy in their work and their arguments. For example, the American Herbartians went to Germany to study with the explicators of Herbart and returned with a mixture of philosophy and psychology that they fashioned into a theory of education. They maintained that education was basically a matter of ethics and that the purpose of education was to produce the proper kind of character. To achieve this aim, it was necessary to follow the laws of psychology. Accordingly, they emphasized two major psychological concepts - interest and apperception - and used them to organize both subject matter and the process of teaching. They explained the development of children in a way that was consistent with their aim of education by employing a notion of recapitulation that maintained that the child traversed through stages much like those that a people traversed as it achieved its civilization. That was a notion the structure of which could be likened to either Hegel's philosophy of history or to G. Stanley Hall's notion of recapitulation. While the popularity of the Herbartians rose and fell quickly, their role as a bridge between philosophy and psychology as the basis of work and inquiry in education is one that has not yet been fully told.

A flurry of psychology texts appeared in the 1890s. These included William James' Principles of Psychology (1890), John Dewey's Psychology (1887), and William Torry Harris' Psychologic Foundations of Education (1898). Although William James moved from psychology to philosophy after the publication of the Principles, many psychologists managed to rid themselves of their philosophical baggage. Some went to work on educational problems or applied their new methods to old problems. Others tried to apply the findings of the new science of the mind to education and expected quick and dramatic results. They were frequently disappointed. Still others saw great possibilities in psychology and promised that all sorts of human problems would be quickly resolved with the data gathered by psychological workers.

A complete account of all who applied psychology to education cannot be given, for that task would require an entire volume. However, a few illustrative sketches of representative figures can be presented. Those who will be considered here are Edward L. Thorndike, Arnold Gesell, Daniel Starch, and William Chandler Bagley. While these men constitute a disparate group, there are also important similarities among them. Each enjoyed a successful career, each produced works that were widely used in education, and each was a member of the young American professoriate that did not earn its academic credentials abroad.

Edward L. Thorndike and the Transfer of Training

The son of a New England clergyman, Thorndike was born in 1874, one year before James opened his demonstration laboratory at Harvard. Twenty years later in a required course in psychology as Wesleyan University, he encountered James' Principles. To compete in a 'prize examination', he had to read certain chapters of the Principles. In an autobiographical statement written some forty years after his first reading of James, he reported that the chapters he had read 'were stimulating, more so than any book that I had read before, and possibly more so than any read since'.[6] He admonished his professor for not using James' work as the course text and set out to study at Harvard with William James.

Thorndike planned to study literature, philosophy, and psychology at Harvard, but psychology soon consumed all his interest and effort. He began a series of experiments in which children were to guess what he was thinking about and, for guessing correctly, they were rewarded with a piece of candy. For reasons that Thorndike did not report, the authorities at Harvard disapproved of his experiments and he had to discontinue them. Unable to work with children, he turned to chickens (we can only wonder about the course American education might have taken had the Harvard authorities allowed Thorndike to work with children). As the now familiar story goes, there was no room for his chickens at Harvard and his landlady frowned on his keeping them in his room. William James, to the delight of his children, came to the rescue and offered his cellar to Thorndike's chickens.

In 1898 Thorndike received an offer from James McKeen Cattell to complete his work in psychology at Columbia University in New York City. When he set out for New York, he carried a basket with his 'two most educated chickens'. He had planned to breed them so that he could 'test the influences of acquired mental traits upon inherited capacity'.[7] The breeding rate of the chickens, he later reported, rendered that 'a foolish plan'. He abandoned his fowl plans and turned to cats and completed his doctoral dissertation, Animal Intelligence. An appointment at the College for Women of Western Reserve University in Cleveland, Ohio, required him to teach education, a subject he had not previously studied. In 1899 he was invited to teach psychology and child study at Teachers College, Columbia University. There he spent his entire career and became one of the outstanding figures in education, educational psychology and the development of tests and measurement.[8]

In collaboration with Robert S. Woodworth, Thorndike published the first of three articles on transfer of training in the May, 1901 issue of the Psychological Review. Whether examined from the vantage point of psychology, educational psychology, or theories of education, the three articles Thorndike and Woodworth published in 1901 on transfer of training must be viewed as significant. Current texts in Educational Psychology not only still include discussions of the transfer issue but also frequently include a discussion of the Thorndike-Woodworth experiments and Thorndike's subsequent work on the transfer problem.

The transfer experiments were important and received almost immediate notice because they related directly to one of the major educational issues of the time. By 1890 there was little doubt that there would be high schools open to all the children of all the people. The major question was Herbert Spencer's: 'What knowledge is of most worth?'. As Spencer and his adherents raised their objections to the classical curriculum, educators had to decide whether to persist in traditional ways or reform the curriculum. They asked: what was to be taught? Latin? Science? they argued whether the high school should prepare its students for college or for life. They asked whether training should be specific or whether general education should be continued. Then, as now, the possibility or impossibility of transfer of training determined how many would answer such questions about the curriculum.

When Thorndike and Woodworth set up experimental situations to determine with precision the extent to which improvement in the one activity would transfer to other kinds of activities, they embarked upon a course that was to change the character of future educational debates. The debates about faculty psychology, mental discipline, and formal discipline would continue, but after Thorndike and Woodworth, the concepts would fall under a new heading - transfer of training or transfer of learning - and the participants in the debate would be required to have either experimental or quantifiable data to support their claims.

The Thorndike-Woodworth studies and those that quickly followed seemed to support the claims of those who were trying to discredit the old psychological doctrines and replace the classical curriculum with one that would be more practical and relevant to students in the first years of the twentieth century. Now there was not only theoretical doubt about transfer and discipline and faculty psychology, but also scientific proof.

Even those who wanted to hold on to old theories and old ways had to deal with the new transfer studies. For example, William C. Bagley, who would later be known for his questions about progressive education, had to admit in 1904 that 'the doctrine of "formal discipline" seems doomed'.[9] He was not, however, to surrender completely. 'Personally', he told the membership of the University of Chicago College of Education Faculty in 1908, 'I believe that those who still cling to the dogma in its original form cannot justify their position; I also believe that those who have entirely cast aside the idea of formal training have done so too hastily'.[10] He had constructed and would continue to construct his own alternative to the old doctrine. He called it the 'ideal'. It was similar to a notion that Charles H. Judd was to call the 'theory of conscious generalization'. Bagley presented and discussed his 'ideal' in The Educative Process (1904) and in Educational Values (1911), texts that were widely used in teacher education classes. In the latter work he reviewed nearly twenty studies on formal discipline from England, America, and Germany, some of which supported his own notion that transfer did occur when students were taught that the 'ideal' embedded in the subject matter at hand should be followed in all situations. In the 1930s Bagley and others were still trying to combat the legacy of the Thorndike-Woodworth experiments. Bagley was then maintaining that Pedro Orata had demonstrated 'beyond a peradventure of a doubt' that 'the "transfer" evidence had not only been overworked but actually abused'.[11] He concluded that Orata had conducted a 'searching analysis' of ninety-nine transfer experiments conducted between 1890 and 1928 which showed that 'the total evidence of these experiments, far from demolishing the theory of mental discipline, actually supports it, although obviously not its earlier naive form'.[12]

Although Orata's work, written under the direction of Boyd H. Bode, may have been an attempt to discredit the ideas and influence of Thorndike, it does nonetheless show how much attention the transfer issue was receiving over twenty-five years after the initial publication of the Thorndike-Woodworth studies. Orata's bibliography on 'transfer of training' shows that nearly a generation after the Thorndike-Woodworth studies, psychologists and educators saw fit to publish between three and four studies a year on the transfer question. Neither the transfer question nor its relationship to the school curriculum had been satisfactorily resolved. Discussion continued. In 1914, Peter Sandiford concluded, from a study of 810 articles, that while transfer was a 'real factor' in education, the amount of transfer that could be expected was usually small.[13] As late as 1953, C. E. Osgood concluded that it was not certain that the old doctrine of formal discipline was invalid.[14] Indeed, Lawrence M. Stolurow's review of 1,700 articles in 1966 showed that for two generations, psychologists and educators had committed slightly over two transfer studies a month.[15]

Comparison of the articles on 'Transfer of Learning' in the last two editions (3rd and 4th) of the Encyclopedia of Educational Research reflects changes in research emphases among educators and psychologists. In the third edition (1960), considerable attention was given to the relationship between transfer and education.[16] The discussion of transfer emphasized its relationship to the more general psychological problem of learning.[17]

The various transfer studies were frequently used to tell educators what they wanted to be told. For instance, in the 1927 NSSE Yearbook, The Foundations and Technique of Curriculum-Construction, Harold Rugg reported a study by Thorndike that:

> showed by measuring carefully the ability of 9,000 tenth-grade pupils before and after taking a year of Latin that one year's study of Latin as now organized does increase one's ability to reason - by a small amount - but that the gain is no larger than that due to the study of other school subjects as now organized.

Rugg observed that

> It is of great importance to find, for example, that bookkeeping, cooking, and sewing increase one's ability to generalize even more in some instances than does the study of the Classics.[18]

To Rugg's dismay, the Advisory Committee of the Classical League devoted only two sentences to Thorndike's investigation. The Report of the Classical League noted that 'the study shows that the amount of growth produced by certain school subjects in the ability measured by the tests varies so slightly that no definite conclusions can be drawn therefrom'.[19] Rather than accept the findings of an extensive study, the committee solicited the judgments of seventy psychologists, psychologists who favored the classics.

Arnold Gesell and the Child Study Movement

Through the work of one of G. Stanley Hall's outstanding students, Arnold Gesell, child-study became an enduring feature of American culture and education. Unlike many of America's early educators and psychologists, Gesell did not hail from the Northeast. He was born in 1880 in Alma, Wisconsin. At age nineteen, he earned a teaching certificate and became football coach and teacher of history, accounting, and a few other subjects at the high school in Stevens Point, Wisconsin. By 1904 he had finished the course at the Stevens Point Normal School and had been awarded a Bachelor of Philosophy degree from the University of Wisconsin. He then set out for Massachusetts to study with G. Stanley Hall at Clark University. In 1906 he was awarded his Ph.D. and moved to Los Angeles where he accepted a position as a principal and assistant professor of psychology at the State Normal School. Soon he was invited to Yale University as a part-time assistant professor of psychology. He accepted the position because it also afforded him the opportunity to pursue a medical degree, a necessity for the kind of work he wanted to undertake. In 1915 he had his M.D. degree and set out to map the entire course of child development. It was an undertaking he had begun in 1911 in the New Haven dispensary which he used as the site for his studies. In time, his work was to be conducted through the Yale Clinic of Child Development and was to have an international reputation.

Hall had once persuaded the Worcester, Massachusetts State Normal School to collect information on children. In a short time, the Normal School had assembled 35,000 observations. Following in the ways of Hall, in 1918 Gesell and his staff undertook a complete mental survey of the children in New Haven's elementary schools. The results of that survey led to the recommendations Gesell prescribed in _Exceptional Children and Public School Policy_. Gesell insisted that the school had to be constantly aware of the principles of mental hygiene, deal with each child not as a member of a class but as an individual, and have as its primary objectives the healthy psychological and physical development of each child.

Gesell found a way to gather data about children that was more reliable than Hall's use of teachers. Gesell developed what he called 'cinemanalysis'. In place of teachers he used a movie camera. For the study of infants he developed a dome which was encased by a one-way vision screen. On the quadrants of the dome, silent cameras moved back and forth to record the behaviour of the subjects. Before Gesell's career ended, he had accumulated nearly fifty-seven miles of film on the behavior of 12,000 children. Many of his books were amply illustrated with photographs of the specific behaviors he discussed. For example, Gesell included 3,200 such photographs in his _An Atlas of Infant Behavior: A Systematic Delineation of the Forms and Early Growth of Human Behavior Patterns_ (1934). The data he collected enabled him to chart the entirety of child development.

Gessell offered a program similar to that of his mentor, Hall, who had earlier celebrated the teacher who ceased to view 'pupils as marionettes to be treated as groups or classes, but as free units, with a bond of sympathy between each of their hearts and his own'.[20] Hall, Gesell and others effectively changed the language of the school business. In place of talk about students' accomplishments in traditional school subjects - reading, writing, arithmetic, history, language, geography - there developed the language which emphasized the need for healthy self-concepts and the well-adjusted child. For example, in _The First Five_

Years of Life, Gesell suggested that 'early reading difficulties would vanish if the natural processes of maturation were given a chance to assert themselves'.[21] The problem of reading could be corrected by paying closer attention to the child's development. When cultural pressures and psychological processes conflicted, the best course, he suggested, was to follow the psychological route. As Gesell put it:

> When culture and child come into conflict, it is time to be mindful of growth factors. Reading is a major cultural goal set up by society in an age which is strongly eye-minded. Important as the goal may be, it cannot be realized through sheer drill and direct pressure. Concessions must be made to the nascent needs and to the pattern of individual development.[22]

For some, the norms Gesell developed were used to allow children to do what they seemed to want to do and to support the belief that all children would learn what they needed to know when they were ready to learn it. For others, Gesell's norms became a source of concern when the children in their charge did not seem to measure up to what Gesell had laid out.

Daniel Starch and Educational Measurement

Like Thorndike and Gesell, Daniel Starch was an early psychologist who did not have to journey to Germany for his training and credentials. Unlike Gesell, he did not even have to journey to the east for a training in psychology. When he was ready to begin graduate study in 1903, he was able to do so in the mid-west where he was born. Like Gesell, he was a native of Wisconsin, having been born in LaCrosse in 1883. He attended the Morningside College in Sioux City, Iowa where he majored in psychology and mathematics, subjects that prepared him to pursue the new booming science, experimental psychology. In 1903, he secured a fellowship from the State University of Iowa where Carl Emil Seashore had been recently appointed professor of psychology. With Seashore, Starch studied psychology and education, and was awarded an M.A. degree in 1904, and a Ph.D. in 1906. He remained at Iowa for one year to serve the customary apprenticeship as an instructor in experimental psychology. He then moved to Massachusetts to serve as an instructor in experimental psychology at Wellesley College and to study experimental psychology at Harvard. In 1908 he left Wellesley to begin a twelve-year tenure at the University of Wisconsin where he began to write several books in which he attempted to apply the findings of the new science to education and to advertising.

Starch's applications of psychology to practical affairs, education and advertising, were very successful. His growing reputation in the psychology of advertising led to his appointment as a lecturer at the Harvard Graduate School of Business in 1919. From that time on, most, though not all, of his professional work was in the field of advertising.

Most of Starch's work in education occurred between 1906 and 1919. In his work in education, he concentrated on the measurement of pupil achievement, the reliability of grading practices, and the determination of the worth of the various school subjects. He also published a text, Educational Psychology, in 1919. For nearly ten years it was the most widely used text in the field, was reprinted thirteen times, and for a time was more widely used than Thorndike's text.

During 1912-13, Starch collaborated with E. C. Elliott in the publication of three articles in the School Review on the reliability of grading in high school English, History and Mathematics. The new well-known Starch-Elliott studies were among the first of their kind. They set out to determine how widely grading practices varied, and their findings consistently revealed that marks assigned to a given paper by different readers varied widely. The wide ranges of variations prompted Starch to write his text, Educational Measurements, in 1916.

While Starch admitted that most educational measurements were still in the experimental stage, he also claimed that 'the need of definite, objective measures of educational products' was sufficiently 'great' to proceed with the work.[23] A year earlier, he had concluded that 'the current movement for measuring school products is one of the three or four most important fields of investigation in the scientific study of educational "programs"'.[24] For Starch, there was no doubt about the propriety of educational measurement. The old pedagogy was to be replaced with 'quantitative studies, objective measurements, and carefully observed facts'. In a statement very much like one made by Thorndike a few years earlier, Starch told his readers that 'any quality or ability of human nature that is detectable is also measureable'.[25] All that educators needed to do was to find better ways to make their measurements and further refine their tests and scales.

There was no need to defend educational measurement. It was an integral part of the daily work of the school. It was either used or mis-used each time any grade or mark was assigned. Moreover, there were 'numerous and momentous problems' in the working of a school that depended upon the assignment of marks. Decisions about 'promotion, retardation, elimination, honors, eligibility for contests and societies, graduation, admission to higher institutions, recommendation for future positions' all depended upon the grades a student had been assigned. Better than or worse than was ascribed to persons or situations by many people many times a day. All sorts of comparative judgments about all sorts of matters were part of life. Educators, Starch believed, should refine their judgments so they could 'express them in terms of known units of a definable character'. He wanted educators to be able to report 'that a pupil can read three words per second of a certain passage and to repeat so and so much of it, that he knows the English meaning of 2,000 Latin words and can translate without error sentences of specified difficulty'. If there were educational 'products or by-products' that could not be judged to exist in some quantity, then, Starch advised, 'we may be suspicious of their actual existence'.[26]

Starch recommended that 'marks on the whole and for large groups of pupils of usual ability should be distributed with a reasonably close conformity to the normal, bell-shaped, probability curve'. He reasoned that since human physical traits and psychological traits to the extent that they had been measured conformed to the probability curve, there was no reason why all marks should not be normally distributed. He acknowledged that there were factors that tended to skew the curve in one direction or the other, but he also claimed that these factors ultimately counterbalanced each other. For example, the elimination of the poor students from schools, especially in the upper grades, and the improved performance of students because of good teaching were often offset by the lower performance of students who did not always employ maximum effort. He also argued that the elimination of the poor student was 'not a cutting off at a definite point of the curve, but rather a smooth shaving off along the entire range'. Grades would then 'be assigned much more justly if they are assigned with reasonably close conformity to the probability distribution'.[27] Though Harold O. Rugg presented data which showed 'that the normal distribution did not hold in some cases, and that many factors affecting marks were not susceptible to an assumption of normality',[28] Starch and others during this period did not cease to urge that all educational data be made to conform to the normal curve.

In his text, Educational Psychology, Starch employed the normal curve to explain the nature of human variation. That the normal curve may only represent how widely distributed variations were and not what they meant to either an individual or a society was not a topic that Starch entertained. To know that human abilities varied in accordance with the normal curve was, for Starch, to know the nature of human variation. To illustrate the nature of human variation, he presented in graphic form a number of different distributions. They included: the memory ability of 173 university students, the ability of 164 university students to cancel A's in one minute, the ability of 164 persons to cancel a specified geometrical figure in a page of figures in one minute, the ability of 135 persons in giving associations to a stimulus word in fifteen seconds, chest measurements of English soldiers, the height of 1,052 women, the head girth of 1,071 boys between the ages of 16 and 19, and the number of heads up in tossing ten pennies 1,000 times. Starch sought to teach future teachers that all distributions of human traits and all human performance approximated a normal distribution.

For Starch, as for many of his contemporaries, waste in education was a major problem, a problem that needed immediate attention. Investigation of teaching practices and pupil performance had led many to believe that while much remained to be learned, they had already learned enough to conclude that improvement was indeed possible. Starch and others found that they could measure time. At times, their measurements were absurd. For example, Starch presented his readers with a passage that is reminiscent of Rabelais. It goes as follows:

> We do not know with any definite assurance what is the most economical amount of time to devote to any one of the school subjects. From such investigations as have been made, we may infer that there is an enormous waste in our educational practices which is indicated by such facts as the following: It has been found by recent tests and measurements that some schools obtain just as good results by devoting only one-half as much time to writing as other schools do. Similar facts have been brought out in the case of reading, arithmetic, and other school subjects. Schools which have devoted as much as 100 minutes a week, or 20 minutes a day, have obtained no better results than other schools devoting 50 minutes a week, or 10 minutes a day, to the same subject. If these facts actually represent the real possibilities, it seems quite obvious that here is an enormous waste in our schools and this waste is far greater than we realize until we make definite calculations of the possible savings of time. If by some means it were possible to save one minute a day for every school day during the eight years of a child's school life, we would be able to save one entire week of school time. If we could save four minutes a day for the same length of time, we would be able to save one month; if we were able to save 18 minutes a day, we would be able to save one-half a school year; and if by more economical methods of learning and distribution of time we were able to save 36 minutes a day for eight years, we would be able to save an entire school year. Such a saving is not impossible; indeed, by a better use of time and more effective methods of learning, it is highly probable. Eighteen minutes a day would mean a reduction of only 4½ minutes in each of four subjects; 36 minutes a day would mean a reduction of only 9 minutes a day in each of four subjects.[29]

Although not enough was known about how students learn to enable educators to shorten the school day and the school year for all students, it was possible, Starch maintained, to effect some reductions for some students. Starch was confident that waste could be eliminated and that economics could be introduced into school. All facets of students' performances could be reduced to differences in either time or amount. As Starch explained, 'we find that on the average the best pupil is able to do the same task from two to twenty-five times as well as the poorest pupils'.[30]

Just as improved methods of teaching based on psychological knowledge about learning promised the ability to save minutes and perhaps years, so did the variability in human abilities make possible the savings of school time. Starch reported that measurement of pupils' abilities in the various school subjects revealed that 'the differences in abilities in school subjects are fully as wide as in special psychological capacities'.[31] Since the wide range of differences was 'probably due primarily to native ability rather than to differences in opportunity, training or environment', a wide range of ability could be expected in every class and in every school. Even after the abilities of the students in the various school subjects had been averaged, there was still a range such that the superior, second and third grade students were nearly equal to the poorest students in the eighth grade. According to Starch, 'this enormous range of ability and the resulting overlapping of successive grades, is probably the most important single fact discovered with reference to education in the last decade'.[32]

Starch argued that in society, adults of superior drive and ability were allowed to compete and earn rewards and that children should be given the same opportunity in school. He also argued that children who performed in a superior fashion in school were also of superior character. He related that:

> Considerable information concerning the character traits of a child may be inferred from his mental and educational test data. If in educational attainment a child is one quartile position above that customary for children of his intelligence quotient, excellent character traits are likely to be present; if his educational attainment accords with that customary for children of his intelligence quotient, average character traits may be inferred; if, however, his educational attainment is one quartile position below that customary for children of his intelligence quotient, poor character traits are probable.[33]

Through psychology, Starch discovered a not very new form of early American Calvinism. Successful people in the society were to be seen as deserving of their success because of their superior character. Those who met with misfortune could be considered to have earned their just reward. Starch's views were, however, consistent with many of his era. For example, in 1908 William H. Allen, the general agent for the New York Association for Improving the Condition of the Poor, proclaimed that 'the modern Diogenes does not go about with a lantern seeking goodness; he looks for efficiency and expects goodness to be thrown in'.[35] For those who believed that people varied only in the amounts of traits they possessed, that may not have seemed unreasonable.

W. C. Bagley and the Science of Education

Like Starch and Gesell, William Chandler Bagley completed his undergraduate education in the midwest. He graduated from the Michigan Agricultural College in 1895, and immediately learned that the 'panic (we now call them recessions) of 1893' created a scarcity of jobs. Unable to find a position that would enable him to practice scientific agriculture, he took a job in a one-teacher school in Garth, Delta County, in the Upper Peninsula of Michigan. According to his biographer, I. L. Kandel, the task of teaching 'inspired him with an ambition to find out more about the principles of education and to inquire whether such principles could not be discovered and established by scientific methods'.[35]

To learn about the new science of the mind, Bagley spent his summer vacation of 1896 at the University of Chicago where he studied psychology, and, under Jacques Loeb, the physiology of the nervous system. He spent another year teaching at Garth, and then enrolled in the University of Wisconsin where he received the Master of Science degree in 1898. There he studied under Joseph Jastrow, who was later to have a syndicated column on psychology in many American newspapers; Michael Vincent O'Shea, who was one of the promoters of child study, and John William Stearns from whom he took work in the Herbartian pedagogy. For his doctoral work, Bagley went to Cornell where he studied psychology and education. From Edward Bradford Titchener, one of Wundt's students, he doubtlessly learned about structuralism and Titchener's objections to functional psychology. However, Bagley himself would later indicate his partiality to functionalism. From the Herbartian, Charles DeGarmo, Bagley took work in the psychologic foundations of education, the science and art of teaching, and philosophy of education.

Bagley was among those who believed that there were laws that governed the educative process, that those laws could be discovered, and that education could be improved by following those laws. In 1905 in The Educative Process, he maintained that there were 'basal principles of the educative process' that could be subverted by even the experienced teacher who had already mastered the techniques of teaching. Therefore, it was necessary that 'an adequate conception of principles based on the best data that science can offer ... be added to a mastery of techniques'. He explained that 'clear and definite notions of the functions of education and of the laws which govern the educative process will do much toward eliminating the waste of time and energy that is involved in the work of the school'.[36]

Bagley offered the view - a view shared by many of his era - that the study of education, or of any other complicated process, initially reveals 'a vast noisy machine, the various parts of which appear to work with little reference to the needs and nature of the whole; not a coordinated system of interacting elements, but a mere aggregation of independent units'. For many centuries, the organic world appeared to be characterized by independent forces and forms, waste of time and energy and absence of relationships until science developed the capability to 'strip the mask from things'. Once the organic world had been revealed, 'the harmonious cooperation of all these factors toward a definite end' was clear.[37]

Through science, investigators had been able to identify the organic world's components. Education also needed to be reduced to its lowest possible terms so that educators could gain control of it and give it proper direction. 'In the study of the concrete problems of education', claimed Bagley, 'we need a guiding principle; we need a formula that will convey every case that is presented; we need to know what education means in its simplest terms'. Without that principle, there was neither a basis for interpretation nor a criterion 'for approval or condemnation'.[38]

In the first years of his career, Bagley believed that psychology would contribute to the development of a science of education. However, he soon changed his view and began to argue that a proper science of education would have to stand on its own. By 1912 he was arguing that education would have to develop its own science independent of other sciences. Writing in the Kansas School Magazine, he indicated that

> It is out of the question to solve satisfactorily the problems of education by deductive inferences from the principles that

> have been worked out in what we call the 'pure' sciences. We cannot, for example, take the principles of psychology and deduce from these conclusions regarding educational problems that will unerringly 'work'. We can get useful hypotheses, but these must be relentlessly subjected to the crucible of actual test under educational conditions. Medicine profited wonderfully by the work that has been done in chemistry and in physiology; and yet the great achievements in medicine have been made since it undertook the experimental study of its own specific problems, in the light of chemical and physiological knowledge, it is true, and yet independently of these basic sciences. Agriculture has made its great progress not by neglecting what chemistry and biology had to teach, but by the experimental investigation of its own problems in the light of these teachings. Education cannot hope to progress rapidly until it has reached a similar point in its development. We must, in a sense, declare our independence, take a scientific method which is our most precious heritage from the basic sciences, and with its aid work out our own salvation.[39]

Bagley believed that if educators would apply the scientific method to the problems of education, 'the naked fact will be revealed'. Then educators would know what to do.

Bagley continued to argue that the problems of education could not be reduced profitably to psychological problems. To attempt to do so was to impose extra-educational abstractions on education - abstractions that promised more than was ever delivered. In 1914 he offered a catalogue of the psychological abstractions that had been unsuccessfully applied to education. He related that:

> Twenty years ago, when I began the study of education, I was convinced its problems could be adequately described, formulated, and solved in terms of nerve cells and fibers. These concepts of physiological psychology had their brief day and added their small mite to educational theory - a day much briefer and a mite smaller than I dreamed of at the time. A little later, experimental psychology, with its distinction between the motor-minded and the eye-minded, held the field. Then genetic psychology, with its culture-epoch-parallelism, came and went in its turn leaving behind it a host of disappointed hopes and a few grains of precious truth. And today a veritable host of abstractions are clamoring for educational content to give them meat and substance ....[40]

Bagley eventually surrendered the notion that psychology could provide the foundation for a science of education, but many held to the mistaken belief that psychology was the proper basis for education. As David C. Berliner and N. L. Gage observed in the 1976 NSSE Yearbook, at the turn of the century 'empirical research, primarily psychological, seemed to be only a few short years from solving the problems of education by providing the scientific underpinning for instructional practice'. However, the marriage of education and psychology turned out to be a 'disappointing marriage'.[41] Some might even say barren. Even the hopeful claims of the behaviourists, the practitioners of a psychology that supposedly freed itself from all sorts of ambiguities and metaphysical assumptions, seem especially with the advantage of hindsight, somewhat sanguine. Certainly the promise that J. B. Watson saw when he wrote his first article about behaviorism in 1913 has not been realized. Some have, as he urged, developed a psychology that 'recognizes no dividing line between man and brute',[42] but most teachers persist in seeing differences between children and pigeons.

The judgments about human beings that the foregoing psychologists supported with their ideas fell on fertile ground. The psychologists simply found data to support what many Americans believed long before the beginnings of modern psychology. For example, Crèvecoeur, in his Letters from an American Farmer, published in 1782, described the 'great metamorphosis' Europeans experienced after their arrival on the American continent. However, he also noted that not all Europeans were equally successful, and he offered his own observations on their differing rates of success:

> From whence the differences arise, I know not; but out of twelve families of emigrants of each country, generally seven Scotch will succeed, nine German, and four Irish. The Scotch are frugal and laborious, but their wives cannot work so hard as the German women, who, on the contrary, vie with their husbands, and often share with them the most severe toils of the field, which they understand better. They have therefore nothing to struggle against but the common casualties of nature. The Irish do not prosper so well; they love to drink and quarrell; they are litigious, and soon take to the gun, which is the ruin of everything. They seem, beside, to labour under a greater degree of ignorance in husbandry than the others; perhaps it is that their industry had less scope and was less exercised at home.[43]

Crèvecoeur explained the differences among the various peoples in terms of the environments from which they came, but the differences he expressed became stereotypes that endured.

Notions about human differences were not confined to politicians and social and behavioral scientists. By the 1920s, such talk was common, part of the popular culture. For example, early in The Great Gatsby, F. Scott Fitzgerald has the host of a small dinner party, Tom Buchanan, Daisy's husband, express his concern for the survival of the white race. Tom asks his guests whether they have read Goddard's Rise of the Colored Empires, and goes on to explain that 'it's a fine book, and everybody ought to read it. The idea is if we don't look out, the white race will be - will be utterly submerged'. He then tried to assure his guests that 'It's all scientific stuff; it's been proved'. Daisy observes that Tom has been turning 'very profound' and the conversation continues.[44]

As educators continued to reflect the prejudices and fears of American society, they placed themselves in a paradoxical position. While they argued that schools were necessary to Americanize the immigrants and thereby create a unified social order, they also claimed that not all people were truly capable of being educated and becoming thoroughly American. For many prospective teachers, that double message must have been confusing. For immigrants and members of minority groups, it was patently unfair.

As shown in this paper, the emphasis on measurement and quantification in both educational and psychological inquiries persisted. For some it was more than an emphasis; it was an obsession. In a letter written to Adelbert Ames in 1949, John Dewey offered his opinion on quantification:

> I have been convinced for a long time that the obsession of psychologists with quantity is both a cause and an

> effect of the backwardness of that subject. A quantitative statement with no theory to determine what is being measured would justify calling the "measuring" of all cracks in the plaster of my wall "science" if it were done with elaborate statistical technique. To hell with it - but unfortunately they hoodooed the Foundations' Directors, who have little idea of what Scientific Method is, joined with a superstitious respect for what they think is science - with an extra big capital letter.[45]

Charles Brauner has characterized educational researchers of this period as 'fact-gathering worker-bees'.[46] We should entertain the notion that this characterization may prove to be inappropriate. Worker-bees have a purpose and they produce honey, a substance that is both nourishing and sticky. We have been left much to review that is sticky.

REFERENCES

[1]Lawrence A. Cremin. The Transformation of the School (New York: Knopf, 1962) p. 85.

[2]Lawrence A. Cremin, 'The Revolution in American Secondary Education, 1893-1918', Teachers College Record, Vol. LVI, No. 6 (March, 1955) p. 296.

[3]Ibid., p. 307.

[4]Ibid.

[5]The American graduate school is not much older than the University's involvement in pedagogical matters. Although Yale decided to grant the Ph.D. degree in 1860 and quickly awarded the first three doctorates earned in an American university, graduate education did not really get underway in a significant manner until 1876 when Johns Hopkins opened. Between the beginnings of Yale's program and Johns Hopkins' opening, twenty-five schools had awarded forty-four graduate degrees. See: Frederick Rudolph. The American College and University (New York: Knopf, 1962), p. 335.

Other schools soon followed the lead of Johns Hopkins. In 1880, Columbia University began graduate work in the political and social sciences, and within a year, the University of Michigan followed suit. In 1890, Harvard and the University of Chicago opened graduate schools of art and sciences. The consequences for college professors were soon evident: publication of scholarship and completion of advanced graduate work were to become requisite for promotion and tenure. A development that helped to shape the model professors of education had to follow, and one that probably encouraged some to engage in educational research. See: Laurence A. Veysey. The Emergence of the American University (Chicago: The University of Chicago Press, 1965), pp. 175-176.

[6]Edward L. Thorndike, 'Autobiography' in Geraldine M. Joncich. Psychology and the Science of Education: Selected Writings of Edward L. Thorndike (New York: Teachers College Press, 1962), p. 28.

[7]Ibid., pp. 29-30.

[8]E. L. Thorndike's Introduction to the Theory of Mental and Social Measurements (1904) is generally accepted to signal the beginning of the application of statistical methods to educational problems in the United States though the

work of Cattell and Galton was known and there was already some teaching of statistics in the American university. However, Harold O. Rugg's Statistical Methods Applied to Education (1917) was the book that was widely used in teacher training courses. According to Walter S. Monroe, Rugg's book 'which dealt with tabulation, averages, variability, rectilinear correlation, the normal frequency curve, and so forth, in easily understood language, began at once to receive wide use ... and served to give thousands of workers in the field of education an elementary but practical knowledge of statistical methods'. See: Walter Scott Monroe. 'Ten Years of Educational Research, 1918-1927', University of Illinois Bureau of Educational Research Bulletin No. 42, University of Illinois Bulletin, Vol. 25, No. 51. 1928, p. 36.

[9]William C. Bagley, 'Ideals Versus Generalized Habits', School and Home Education, Vol. CCIV, No. 3 (November, 1904) p. 102.

[10]William C. Bagley, 'The School's Responsibility for Developing the Controls of Conduct', The Elementary School Teacher, Vol. VIII, No. 7 (March, 1908), p. 356.

[11]William C. Bagley, Education, Crime and Social Progress (New York: The Macmillan Co., 1931) p. 126.

[12]William C. Bagley, Education and Emergent Man (New York: Thomas Nelson and Sons, 1934) p. 37.

[13]Peter Sandiford, 'Transfer of Learning' in Walter S. Monroe (ed.) Encyclopedia of Educational Research, rev. ed. (New York: The Macmillan Co., 1950) p. 1312.

[14]C. E. Osgood, Method and Theory in Experimental Psychology (New York: Oxford University Press, 1953).

[15]Lawrence M. Stolurow. Psychological and Educational Factors in Transfer of Training: Section 1. (Urbana, Illinois: Training Research Laboratory, 1966).

[16]J. M. Stephens, 'Transfer of Learning' in Chester W. Harris (ed.). Encyclopedia of Educational Research. 3rd ed. (New York: The Macmillan Co., 1960), pp. 1541-1452.

[17]Herbert J. Klausmeier and J. Kent Davis, 'Transfer of Learning' in Robert L. Ebel (ed.). Encyclopedia of Educational Research, 4th ed. (Toronto: Collier-Macmillan, 1970), pp. 1483-1491.

[18]Harold O. Rugg, 'Three Decades of Mental Discipline: Curriculum Making via National Committees' in Guy Montrose Whipple (ed.). The Foundations and Techniques of Curriculum Construction: The Twenty-Sixth Yearbook of the National Society for the Study of Education (Bloomington, Illinois: Public School Publishing Co., 1926), p. 61.

[19]Quoted in Rugg, 'Three Decades of Mental Discipline', p. 62.

[20]G. Stanley Hall, 'Child-Study and its Relations to Education', in Charles Strickland and Charles Burgess (eds.). Health, Growth, and Heredity: G. Stanley Hall on Natural Education (New York: Teachers College Press, 1965), p. 87.

[21]Arnold Gesell, et al. The First Five Years of Life (New York: Harper and Brothers, 1940), p. 313.

[22]Ibid., pp. 313-314.

[23]Daniel Starch. Educational Measurements (New York: The Macmillan Co., 1916), p.1.

[24]Daniel Starch, 'The Measurement of Efficiency in Reading', Journal of Educational Psychology, Vol. VI, No. 1 (January, 1915), p. 1.

[25] Starch, Educational Measurements, p. 2. Thorndike's statement, made in 1914, was: 'If a thing exists, it exists in some amount; and if it exists in some amount, it can be measured'. It was, according to Douglas E. Scates, made at the First Annual Conference on Educational Measurements at Indiana University in the Spring of 1914. It was published in the Bulletin of the Extension Division, Indiana University, Vol. XII, No. 10 (September, 1914), p. 37. In 1918, Thorndike gave the statement a different form: 'Whatever exists at all exists in some amount'. See: Douglas E. Scates, 'Fifty Years of Objective Measurement and Research in Education', Journal of Educational Research, Vol. XLI, No. 4 (December, 1947), p. 247.

[26] Starch, Educational Measurements, pp. 2-3.

[27] Ibid., p. 12.

[28] Ann Z. Smith and John E. Dobbin, 'Marks and Marking Systems' in Chester W. Harris (ed.). Encyclopedia of Educational Research. 3rd ed. (New York: The Macmillan Co., 1960), p. 484.

[29] Daniel Starch, Educational Psychology (New York: The Macmillan Co., 1919), pp. 3-4).

[30] Ibid., p. 29.

[31] Ibid., p. 33.

[32] Ibid., p. 39. Starch's emphasis.

[33] Ibid., pp. 45-46.

[34] William H. Allen. Efficient Democracy (New York: Dodd, Mead and Co., 1908), p. 6.

[35] I. L. Kandel. William Chandler Bagley: Stalwart Educator (New York: Teacher College Press, 1961), p. 63.

[36] William C. Bagley. The Educative Process (New York: The Macmillan Co., 1905), pp. v-vi.

[37] Ibid., p. 2.

[38] Ibid., p. 22.

[39] William C. Bagley, 'A Plea for the Scientific Study of Educational Problems', Kansas School Magazine, Vol. 1, No. 2 (February, 1912), p. 54.

[40] William C. Bagley, 'Fundamental Distinctions Between Liberal and Vocational Education, II', NEA Proceedings (1914), p. 164.

[41] David C. Berliner and N. L. Gage, 'The Psychology of Teaching Methods', N. L. Gage (ed.). The Psychology of Teaching Methods: The Seventy-fifth Year-book of the National Society for the Study of Education, Part I (Chicago: University of Chicago Press, 1976), p.1.

[42] J. B. Watson, 'Psychology as the Behaviorist Views It', Psychological Review, Vol. XX (1913) reprinted in Wayne Dennis (ed.). Readings in the History of Psychology (New York: Appleton-Century-Crofts, Inc., 1948) p. 457.

[43] Hector St. John De Crèvecoeur. Letters from an American Farmer (London: J. M. Dent and Sons, 1962), p. 62.

[44] F. Scott Fitzgerald. The Great Gatsby (Charles Scribner's Sons, 1952) pp. 11-12.

[45] John Dewey to Adelbert Ames, May 27, 1949 in Hadley Cantril (ed.). The Morning Notes of Adelbert Ames, Jr. (New Brunswick, New Jersey: Rutgers University Press, 1960), p. 191. Dewey had, of course, offered his opinions on the use and interpretation of tests much earlier. In 1922, he tried to point out

'that the current reception of the results of mental testing proves the extent to which we are given to judging and treating individuals not as individuals but as creatures of a class, a quantitative class which covers up truly individualized traits. Our mechanical, industrialized civilization is concerned with averages, with percents. The mental habit which reflects this social scene subordinates education and social arrangements to stratifications based on averaged gross inferiorities and superiorities. We accept standards of judging individuals which are based on the qualities of mind and character which win under existing social conditions conspicuous success'. See: John Dewey, 'Individual Equality and Superiority', The New Republic (December 13, 1922) reprinted in Joseph Ratner (ed.). Education Today (Westport, Connecticut: Greenwood Press, 1969), p. 171.

[46] Charles J. Brauner. American Educational Theory (Englewood Cliffs, New Jersey: Prentice-Hall, Inc., 1964), pp. 139-140.

THE MEANING OF INTELLIGENCE

Bernard Norton
Lecturer, Department of Astronomy and History of Science
University of Leicester

ABSTRACT

This paper offers a revised explanation of the origins and subsequent career of Charles Spearman's general-factor theory of intelligence. It presents Spearman not so much as a descendent of the positivist Karl Pearson (from whom he borrowed the apparatus of mathematical statistics), as a faithful follower of the idealist trend in German psychology (which he took from his teacher Wilhelm Wundt).

****

It's not often that one gets two chances to get something right. Occasionally though, one does, and this paper is a second attempt to produce a decent account of Charles Spearman (1865-1945) and his theory of intelligence - a theory which implied that there was some real existent that IQ tests measured, a theory which seems to have stood the test of time.[1]

I wrote my first paper on Spearman partly because his theory - known variously as the 'central' or 'general' factor theory, or, more simply, as the theory of 'g' - seems to have been so influential, and partly because of the philosophical interest of his labours. Spearman was one of the first psychologists to take up the new methodology of mathematical statistics developed by Karl Pearson in the late 19th century, and we know that Pearson saw his new methodology as the very embodiment of Machian positivism, as a device that could and would transform the social and human sciences into disciplines that were both mathematical and purged of all metaphysical content.[2] I wanted to know whether the transference of the formalism of statistics went hand in hand with a transference of the philosophical intentions of the author of the new methods.

My first paper was the subject of some critical comment. Some of this led me to realise that my view of Spearman was incorrect in places, unbalanced in parts, and a little fuzzy almost everywhere. Hence this paper aims to correct, balance and clarify. It proceeds as follows. First: I shall offer a reminder of the nature of Spearman's theory. Second: I shall detail my original explanations of Spearman's

(a) constructing the theory in the first place, and (b) defending it so furiously in the teeth of solid criticism, notably from Godfrey Thomson. Third and last: I shall respond to criticism of (a) and (b) above, and, in so doing, hope to present an improved view.

Spearman's theory

Spearman's theory appeared in 1904, and was later described by him as having in some sense fallen out of observed data. The data in question comprised a set of intercorrelations, giving mathematical values for the relationships between the test scores of a number of subjects on various tests.[3] The data used by Spearman in 1904 can be seen below.

TABLE 1

	Classics	French	English	Math.	Discrim	Music
Classics	--	0.83	0.78	0.70	0.66	0.63
French	0.83	--	0.67	0.67	0.65	0.57
English	0.78	0.67	--	0.64	0.54	0.51
Math.	0.70	0.67	0.64	--	0.45	0.51
Discrim.	0.66	0.65	0.54	0.45	--	0.40
Music	0.63	0.57	0.51	0.51	0.40	--

Table 1. Taken from Spearman's 1904 paper. For a demonstration of how Spearman's theory leads to an expectation of hierarchy, see W. Brown and G. Thomson, Essentials of Mental Measurement (Cambridge, 1921), 153-163.

In Table 1 we see the intercorrelations found (after applying certain 'correction' methods) between the scores of the members of a group of twentytwo boys (aged 9.5 to 13.7 years) from a 'high class preparatory school' near Oxford. As may be seen, the tests which Spearman set up or monitored, ranged from mathematics to sensory discrimination, and the various figures give the correlation coefficients connecting the scores of a group of subjects in the various tests. Thus for example, the figure 0.83 gives the measure of correlation between performance in Classics and performance in French. If we suppose, as Spearman did, that test results are determined by two factors - by a 'general' factor, tested in different degrees in different tests and by a factor specific to the test in hand - and that the distribution of specifics is an independent one (in other words, that an individual's having one specific in good measure is no guide as to the degree of his possession of any other factor), then we would expect just the hierarchy of test scores to which Table 1 approximates. That is to say, the correlations may be arranged so that they form a table everywhere diminishing as we move from left to right, and from top to bottom. Moreover, if we take any two adjacent columns, or any two adjacent rows, we find that the ratio between adjacent elements is the same for all pairs of elements in any two columns or any two rows. These predictions can be easily derived from Spearman's theoretical assumptions by using the calculus of partial correlations, notably as developed by Pearson's one-time pupil G. Udny Yule (1871-1951). Naturally, Spearman did not expect every observed table of correlations to fit the criteria just laid out, but, rather, that whenever the tests involved were not closely similar, deviations from perfect hierarchy would be of magnitudes ascribable to sampling error. Much of Spearman's defence of the theory, starting with his joint paper with Bernard Hart in 1912, discussed the erection of suitable criteria for adjudication in this area.[4]

To summarise, Spearman offered a theory of mental functioning which is perhaps best thought of in terms of an engineering analogy.[5] According to Spearman, the mind contains a 'central' or 'general' factor (motor), which can only operate when harnessed to some specific factor (tool-attachment) appropriate to the mental (engineering) task in hand. The overall performance of the mind (machine) is most strongly determined by the strength of the person's central factor (the machine's motor's horsepower). From 1914 onwards, Spearman was prepared to identify this mental horsepower with the results of the IQ tests so recently developed in France by Binet and Simon.[6] In so doing, he effectively reified intelligence, and opened up the way for numerous sociobiologists, from Burt to Jensen, to discuss the hereditary basis of this reified intelligence.[7] In short, Spearman proved a theory of intelligence which offered an account of what it was that the new tests measured. He enabled psychologists to point to an impressive-looking mathematical structure and simultaneously to deny that intelligence was just and only what IQ tests measured. After Spearman, the tests could be seen as estimators of a real quality. Not everybody immediately accepted Spearman's view of matters. In particular, Godfrey Thomson pointed out, time and again, that, although Spearman's theory implied a hierarchy, the reverse inference was invalid: there were other theories of intelligence, notably Thomson's theory of 'mental bonds', that led to an expectation of hierarchy. Spearman, in consequence, became extremely concerned to show the virtue of his own theory and the unsatisfactory quality of Thomson's, and from 1916 to 1939, the organs of British psychology were laden with the exchanges of these two.[8] It is generally held that Spearman emerged the victor - at least in the sense that he was able to gather the larger body of sympathisers. But, from any standpoint, the Thomson-Spearman debate must be seen as one of the most bizarre episodes in the history of modern science. Both theories (Thomson's theory of bonds, and Spearman's theory) made just one prediction, which was in both cases the same - namely that test scores would exhibit hierarchy. It was not a dispute that a Popperian would appreciate!

Why did Spearman propose the theory and defend it so keenly? And how did Spearman use statistics?

When I came to try and answer these questions, I soon found that Spearman was no follower of Pearson's Machian philosophy of science. This is made clear by numerous discussions of the 'central factor' which make it clear that, for Spearman at least, 'g' was not just some convenient instrumentalist's shorthand but, rather a definite entity. As early as 1912, for example,[9] we may find him referring to 'g' as some fund of 'mental energy'. And, as the years went by, Spearman expanded this interpretation of 'g'. By the time he came to identify 'g' with that which was measured by the new Binet tests, Spearman held that his results showed that 'the intelligence employed in any mental performance must be analysed into two factors'.[10]

> The one is different for every different kind of performance or test; it seems to be identifiable with the neural structure in the brain specifically subserving that particular performance. But besides this specific factor, there is also a general one, always the same whatever the performance; this general factor in ability seems to be represented physiologically by the free energy of the whole cortex of the brain, or some still wider neural region ...

This, however, was about as far as Spearman felt able to go. His general factor was, in some sense, a measure of mental energy - of that he felt sure - but he was never able to go much deeper than that, never able to point to specific electric currents for example.[11] For present purposes however, this failure of articulation is unimportant: what is important and interesting is the way in which Spearman was so cheerfully able to appropriate and deploy Pearson's new statistical calculus whilst totally ignoring the philosophical precepts which its author had meant it to embody. For Pearson, talk of 'energy' along Spearman's lines was the purest metaphysics - just the sort of thing that Pearson had developed statistics in order to dispel.

The finding that Spearman was no positivist was not wholly surprising to me, nor yet was it unwelcome, for it meant that the answers to questions about the origin and defence of Spearman's views yield some indication of his 'true' position. Once again, I reflected, it might be possible to show that a work of 'neutral' and 'objective science' was in fact a reflection of some deeply held social or philosophical position.[12] If Kepler had been a neoplatonist, what indeed might Spearman have been?

It now seems to me that, in my enthusiasm, I tended to conflate the origins and defence of Spearman's theory, and that I ended up offering an argument that ran along the following lines.

(1) We know very little about Spearman's early life, except that which may be gathered from his autobiography.[13] This tells us that Spearman nurtured an early and deep hatred for associationism, which, he felt, led on inexorably to the (to him) repellent philosophy of hedonism.

(2) In a second and later part of his work, Spearman developed an explanatory scheme for human cognition characterised by what he referred to as 'noegenetic principles', namely[14]

(a) 'Any lived experience tends to evoke immediately a knowing of its character and experiences'.

(b) 'The mentally presenting of any two or more characters tends to evoke immediately a knowing of relation between them'.

(c) 'The presenting of any character together with any relation tends to evoke a knowing of the correlative character'.

(3) As these principles were recognised (by, e.g. MacDougall) as principles appropriate to the holder of anti-reductionist, anti-associationist, 'active mind' viewpoints,[15] and as Spearman was later to identify 'g' as the energy involved in noegenetic synthesis (which, for Spearman, was the fundamental aspect of all cognition), then did it not make sense to suppose that both the creation and the defence of 'g' were due primarily to a desire to stamp out associationism and to replace it with an active-mind standpoint?[16]

In short, I more or less suggested that 'g' was developed by Spearman, and almost fanatically defended by him because it was the central fund of energy in an anti-associationistic view of mind. At the same time I argued that an already attractive theory (of 'g') became doubly attractive to Spearman when he realised that it had eugenic potential. He was not slow to point out that the theory of'g' opened up the prospect of an 'objective' linear ordering of the population in respect of their fitness to vote and to reproduce.[17]

Critical comments

I received several helpful comments on all of this, the most interesting ones coming from A. D. Lovie and Steve Sharp. Lovie suggested that I had overplayed the influence of eugenics on Spearman's thought, and that I might have underestimated the influences of Spearman's old mentor Wundt, and of Lehmann. Sharp, in a characteristically acute paper,[18] suggested that it was implausible to attribute Spearman's furious defence of 'g' to the role played by 'g' in noegenetic schemes of cognition as

(a) The attacks of Thomson began before the articulation of noegenetic principles, and

(b) 'g' and Spearman's view of cognition were not, in logic, conjoined.

On the other hand, Sharp argued, one might explain Spearman's behaviour in terms of his evident desire to be top dog in psychology: if 'g' were allowed to slip into the role of being just another theory, then its author would lose his magisterial position in British psychology. No wonder he fought Thomson so long and so hard. Influence, ego and power, according to Sharp, were the factors lying behind Spearman's relentless defence of his theory. It was over-idealistic to suppose, as I had done, that everything might be attributed to Spearman's anti-associationistic metaphysics.

Thoughts in response to these criticisms

Lovie's point about Spearman and eugenics must be granted immediately. Like many scientists of his time, Spearman was not slow to draw attention to the eugenic potential of his work. But, when one examines the pattern of his productions and interests, one finds there nothing to indicate the presence of eugenic ideology as a driving force. There was none of that practical concern with mental testing and social organisation that characterised, say, a Cyril Burt. Spearman, first and last, wished to uncover the architecture of the mind - to show the principles according to which our mental contents are constructed.[19] I shall shortly return to Lovie's remarks upon Wundt.

Sharp's suggestions, it seems to me, show the necessity of differentiating clearly between the contexts of discovery and of justification. Sharp, surely, is absolutely correct in discerning a degree of egomania in Spearman's defence of 'g' against Thomson. Spearman was a man capable, in all seriousness, of sitting down and writing a history of psychology in which historical figures were appraised on a basis of how closely their ideas approximated to those of his own.[20] Sharp's other point, namely that the defence of 'g' predates the articulation of the theory of noegenesis, must stand.

On the other hand, against Sharp, I would like to suggest that while it is obviously profitable to explain Spearman's defence of 'g' in terms of egomania, it is implausible to suppose that the same egomania can be invoked to explain the genesis of 'g'. For such a task, pride alone is logically insufficient, we must look for prejudice too (especially if we take Burt's point that Spearman's 'raw' data were not at all suggestive of the theory).[21] Did Spearman's proposal of 'g' derive from metaphysical sentiments? May it not have been the case that, all along, he was driven by some vision of 'g' as a measure of the mind's creative force, even if the articulation of the specific noegenetic doctrines came somewhat later on in his career? Certainly, several points seem to indicate that there may be some substance in such a suggestion.

(i) Such a tendency would place Spearman in line with the contemporary and influential Ward/Stout approach to psychology.[22]

(ii) It fits in with Spearman's 1912 paper (written well before the articulation of the doctrines of noegenesis), in which Spearman argued for the plausibility of his theory by presenting evidence in favour of a 'common fund of intellective energy' acting through a 'specific disposition' appropriate for each mental act.[23]

(iii) It fits in with other points made in 1912, when Spearman spoke of a movement which would reduce the distance between 'individual psychology' and the rest of psychology: he wrote

> many of us are looking forward to the day when psychological textbooks will become less exclusively preoccupied with sensations and epistemology, but turn rather to appreciating the mind or soul as the agent in conduct. If this hope is realised, the general factor or common fund of intellective energy - with its intimate bearing on every kind of intellectual process and above all, on 'attention' - seems bound to take a prominent place.[24]

To me, at any rate, this last quotation does seem strongly to suggest that 'g' was all along seen as the measure of a creative, non-associationistic mind. This, returning to Lovie's points, would not be surprising in the light of Spearman's reverence for his old master Wundt.[25] Wundt, at last, is being rescued from the image - as a positivist - given him by Tichener, and, if Kurt Danziger's ideas are taken to heart, should be seen quite clearly as an anti-positivist, as one whose 'immersion in the current of German idealism is so complete that it hardly requires any special documentation'.[26] Wundt's debts, Danziger argues, lay with Leibniz, Herbart and Kant:

> An examination of Wundt's work, most of which remains untranslated, shows clearly that he explicitly rejected the British psychological traditon of mental and individual atomism and advocated a psychology of 'apperception' which emphasised the constructive rather than the receptive nature of the mind and the irreducibility of mental and social formations. [27]

Danziger's invitation enables us to view Spearman's teacher Wundt in a new light. It certainly does seem that we here have elements which, when put together, show a picture of Spearman as something of a Wundtian anti-positivist, happy to use statistics, but in support of a theory of 'g', which, all along, had a valued interpretation as a measure of the energy of the mind or soul, and not simply as some statistical abstraction.

Such a picture helps us resolve the problem which Sharp's analysis of the Thomson-Spearman debate leaves unanswered - namely the problem of the genesis of 'g'. At the same time, we must surely grant Sharp's point that Spearman's furious defence of his theory, in the longest and most prominent debate in recent British psychology, must be seen in relation to Spearman's egotistical approach to psychology. Power, influence and vanity were important in the context of justification.

REFERENCES

[1] These and other points, I hope, were all brought out in the opening sections of my 'Charles Spearman and the general factor in intelligence: genesis and interpretation in the light of sociopersonal considerations', Journal for the History of the Behavioral Sciences, 15 (1979), 142-154.

[2]For details, see B. Norton, 'Karl Pearson and statistics: the social origins of scientific innovation', Social Studies of Science 8 (1978). 3-34. See also, Karl Pearson, The Grammar of Science, London (1892).

[3]C. Spearman, ' "General Intelligence", objectively determined and measured' American Journal of Psychology, 15 (1904), 201-292.

[4]See B. Hart and C. Spearman, 'General ability, its existence and nature' British Journal of Psychology, 5 (1912) 51-84.

[5]Such an anology was not foreign to Spearman's own writings - though, as we shall see, it was an analogy. He was no mechanist.

[6]See C. Spearman, 'The measurement of intelligence', Eugenics Review 6 (1914-1915), 312-313.

[7]An early example of this is C. Burt, 'Experimental tests of general intelligence' British Journal of Psychology, 3 (1909), 94-177.

[8]An indication of the extent of the debate may be obtained from Helen M. Walker, Studies in the History of Statistical Method, Baltimore (1931); see chapter 6.

[9]Op cit. (note 4).

[10]Spearman, op cit. (note 6), 313.

[11]In this feature of his work, Spearman, of course, resembled Freud. For a discussion see R. Fancher Psychoanalytic Psychology: the Development of Freud's Psychology, New York (1973); see chapter 3.

[12]I attempted such an analysis for Pearson in Norton op cit., (note 2).

[13]See Spearman's autobiographical piece in C. Murchison (ed.) A History of Psychology in Autobiography, Worcester, Mass., (1930), Vol. 1, 299-334. I have consulted the British Psychological Society's archival holdings on Spearman, but they yield little of relevance to his early years.

[14]These were most clearly laid out in C. Spearman, The Nature of 'Intelligence' and the Principles of Cognition, London, (1923).

[15]See, e.g., W. MacDougall, The Energies of Men, London, (1935), 20.

[16]See Norton, op cit. (note 1).

[17]Ibid., 149-154.

[18]See S. Sharp, 'Much ado about nothing: An evaluation of the Thomson-Spearman debate' forthcoming.

[19]This is shown clearly by Spearman, op cit. (note 14).

[20]C. Spearman, Psychology down the Ages, 2 vols. London (19).

[21]See C. Burt, 'The two-factor theory' British Journal of Statistical Psychology, 2 (1949) 151-179.

[22]See D. W. Hamlyn, 'Bradley, Ward and Stout', in B. B. Wolman (ed.) Historical Roots of Contemporary Psychology, New York, (1968).

[23]Spearman, op cit. (note 4). See p.70.

[24]Ibid. See p.77.

[25]For details, see Spearman, op cit. (note 13).

[26]See, for example, K. Danziger, 'The positivist repudiation of Wundt', Journal for the History of the Behavioural Sciences, 15 (1979), 205-230.

[27] Quoted from one of Danziger's forthcoming essays on Wundt. The claim that there is significant similarity between Spearman and his master Wundt is entirely my own. It is a claim for which Danziger bears no responsibility. I hope I have not used his excellent ideas improperly.

GODFREY THOMSON AND THE CONCEPT OF INTELLIGENCE

Stephen A. Sharp
Research Fellow
Godfrey Thomson Unit for Educational Research
University of Edinburgh

ABSTRACT

The paper discusses an incongruity between two aspects of Godfrey Thomson's work. First, he was an early advocate of comprehensive education and argued against totally different educational arrangements provided as a result of performance in a selective examination. Similarly, he was an implacable opponent of the concept of general ability, preferring instead a theory of intelligence based on overlapping group factors, a view which is compatible with his emphasis on educational provision for ability of different types not different levels. Secondly, however, he was the author of the Moray House Tests whose use in the educational system was as a selective mechanism determining the subsequent type and amount of education provided for each child, a practice which Thomson opposed. Since the Moray House tests were more extensively used by LEAs than any other test, it is reasonable to argue that Thomson contributed significantly toward the establishment of an educational administration of which he disapproved. The paper traces the root of this conflict to the social and educational policies which constrained the implementation of Thomson's ideas. In doing so, it also notes that the data to support such an argument must be sought outside, as well as inside, Thomson's published works.

****

Godfrey Thomson was Professor of Education at the University of Edinburgh from 1925 until 1951. In view of his prominence in the development of British psychometrics and educational psychology, there has been surprisingly little discussion of his work in the 24 years since his death. Despite the central importance of his Moray House Tests in making intelligence testing an accepted aspect of British educational policy[1] and despite the contribution of his work on the factorial structure of intelligence, especially his differences with Charles Spearman,[2] the secondary literature on Thomson consists only of the work of Vernon,[3] Robertson,[4] Paterson[5] and Bell.[6] Yet there are aspects of Thomson's work which are highly interesting and which throw new light on the relationship between educational theory and practice; indeed, Thomson is unique in this respect in that he made formative contributions not only to theoretical aspects of the study of intelligence but also to the process of establishing testing as an integral part of the educational system of local authorities throughout the United Kingdom in the 1920s and 1930s. This paper concentrates on the relationship between Thomson's concept of intelligence and the diversity of educational ideas held by Thomson and others between the first and second World Wars.

In common with many educationists, Thomson began his academic training in another subject. Born in Carlisle in 1881, his education at school was weighted towards natural science and his degree at Armstrong College, situated in Newcastle-upon-Tyne but then part of the University of Durham, specialised in mathematics and physics. Following this, he spent the academic years 1904-6 in Strasburg (then part of Germany) where he obtained his doctorate, summa cum laude, in mathematical physics. Many of the famous names of British education spent time in Germany but, unlike Spearman, Burt and Valentine, Thomson showed no interest in psychology at the time and his autobiography[7] makes no mention of any contact with German psychologists.

On his return to Britain, Thomson took a lecturing post at Armstrong College, being required to do this or its equivalent under the terms of the grants on which he had studied. He equipped himself for lecturing on education by becoming an external student at London University, where he became familiar with the work of Herbart, and spent one summer[8] at Cambridge with C. S. Myers. His interests focused, understandably in view of his background, on psychophysics, in which he published his first psychological articles; also on the statistical theory of ability, where he encountered the work of Charles Spearman.

The contribution made by Spearman has been discussed elsewhere[9] and only necessary details will be given here since Spearman is not the subject of this paper. Essentially, Spearman's view was that intelligence may be considered as a homogenous sort of mental energy, of which each person has more or less, and which may be interchangeably applied to the performance of cognitive tasks. Spearman also held that there are specific abilities for each task, which are independent if the tasks are not too similar, and which account for intra-individual variations. Spearman had used the newly-developed calculus of partial correlation to derive from his theory a prediction called 'hierarchical arrangement',[10] which he duly proceeded to verify from experimental data.[11]

Thomson's first opposition to Spearman's work, which comprised Thomson's first publication on anything relevant to intelligence or education, centred around the point that although Spearman's theory predicted 'hierarchical arrangement', the verification of the prediction did not prove the truth of the theory, since other theories might make the same prediction. Thus Thomson's initial reply to Spearman carried the title 'A Hierarchy Without a General Factor'.[12] In it, Thomson used dice to demonstrate the possibility of a system which generates a 'hierarchical arrangement' by means of relationships between groups of tests, without having any relationship common to all the tests, and hence having no general factor. This paper was purely empirical and contained no psychology. Thomson concluded,

> Let me therefore reiterate that all I have shown is that Professor Spearman's calculations are incapable of discriminating between a General Factor and overlapping Group Factors.[13]

By 1919, however, Thomson was beginning to work his purely logical objection into a theory of ability to rival Spearman's:

> The mind, in carrying out an activity such as a mental test, has two levels at which it can operate. The elements of activity at the lower level are entirely specific; but those at the higher level are such that they may come into play in more than one kind of activity, in more than one mental test. These elements are assumed to be additive like dice, and each to act on the 'all or none' principle, not being in fact further divisible.

> The difference between the two levels may be physiological, as between cortex and spinal cord, or it may be the difference between conscious and non-conscious, or what not.[14]

Later, Thomson ceased to speak of 'elements of activity' and referred instead to 'bonds' which constitute the mind and which are called upon in the performance of tasks and sampled by mental tests. One of the striking aspects of Thomson's side of the debate with Spearman was the lack of attention which he devoted to the idea of 'bonds', his discussion of which never runs to more than a few lines:

> What the 'bonds' of the mind are, we do not know. But they are fairly certainly associated with the neurones of nerve cells of our brains, of which there are probably around ten thousand million in each normal brain. Thinking is accompanied by the excitation of these neurones in patterns. The simplest patterns are instinctive, the more complex ones acquired. Intelligence is possibly associated with the number and complexity of the patterns which the brain can (or could) make.[15]

Nevertheless, however scanty the discussion of 'bonds', it is clear that for Thomson they provided a theory just as capable of explaining individual differences in intelligence as was the notion of general ability for Spearman. In addition to the 'bonds', Thomson thought of 'sub-pools' within which the connections between the 'bonds' were closer and more integrated than in general and which correspond to special talents such as, for example, in music and mathematics. Individual differences in general intelligence could then be interpreted as variations in the number of 'bonds' present in the mind and/or as the number and complexity of their interconnections.

At the educational level, Thomson's opposition to Spearman's position centred around his view that a single homogenous general ability, while sufficient to describe the potential of any one given individual, is not suitable for comparing individuals since it takes account only of differences in the quantities of their intelligences and ignores possibly vital differences in their qualities. As Thomson put it quite early in his debate with Spearman:

> In other words general ability, if possessed by any individual, need not be psychologically of the same nature as any general ability possessed by another individual. Everyone has probably known men who were good all round, but Jones may be a good all round man for different reasons from those which make Smith good all round.[16]

The recognition not only of specific abilities of different types, but also of general abilities of different types appears therefore to have been important for Thomson. It may seem strange then that such a man, who devoted so much effort towards demonstrating the inadequacy of the concept of general ability, should also turn out to be the author of a method of intelligence testing designed expressly for use in educational selection, a method whose main features were the administration of exactly the same questions to all children and the representation of each child's educational fitness by a single number emenable to statistical manipulation such as the calculation of age allowances. It would seem at least at first glance, that Spearman's position would have been more compatible with this view of educational fitness than Thomson's, which would lead one to expect profile, rather than scalar, test scores, and it is worth inquiring more deeply into how Thomson came to regard this approach to testing as being important enough to occupy a considerable part of his working life.

Thomson certainly had reasons for being interested in improving the process of educational selection. Born himself into poor circumstances, he was able to attain a high level of education only through the award of various grants and scholarships; and he was concerned that others in the same position should be given every chance to display their ability in competition for such awards.[17] In particular, the possibility that talented schoolchildren in remote areas of Northumberland were being denied educational opportunities by exclusion from the junior scholarship examination led to Thomson's first work on intelligence tests.[18]

Logically, then, there is no incompatibility between Thomson's objection to general ability and his interest in the scalar measurement of intelligence. But there remains an element of incongruity in his simultaneous[19] rejection of general intelligence precisely because of its homogeneity and his striving to develop a tool of measurement whose results were expressed in exactly this form. His stress on the integrative nature of the mind and his view, stemming from his theory, that intelligence tests could be made to sample a wide range of bonds, led him to accept from the outset that IQ was perfectly legitimate as an overall <u>description</u> of mental capacity and, in principle, was a valid alternative view of the <u>nature</u> of intelligence also. But his educational objections to it in the latter role, plus the fact that the tests were expressly designed for educational use, still make it seem somewhat surprising that Thomson and not Spearman should produce this type of test.[20]

The interpretation to be proposed in this paper is that it was a reflection of the disparity between the role he advocated for selection in the educational system and the role which selection was actually playing in British education as it confronted him in the 1920s, 1930s and early 1940s. Whereas Thomson would have preferred to see an educational administration which allowed ample opportunity for the identification and encouragement of different types of scholastic ability, as well as of specific talents, he found in fact an administration based on the notion of different schools for children of different abilities, as assessed by an examination at age eleven. Whereas he would have preferred the various streams to be kept physically together so as to facilitate transference from one to another in the light of the child's performance, he found that the various arrangements for education after age eleven were separately housed and that the resulting difficulty of transferring children gave the examination a more definitive role than he envisaged, as well as stressing quantitative differences in intelligence at the expense of qualitative. Therefore if the view of intelligence implicit in the Moray House tests conflicts to some extent with Thomson's preferred theory of the intellect it is because the former, unlike the latter, was subject to the empirical constraints of the educational system within which it had to work.

We may begin, then, by examining what Thomson saw as the educational objective of testing in general and of the Moray House series in particular. On this he was quite clear, writing that:

> The object ... of these tests is to improve the selection of children for different forms of education (academic, technical, vocational, etc.) in the belief that individual happiness, and the good of the community, are both furthered if the kind of education and ultimately of life-work to which the child is directed are such as his (or her) inborn abilities enable him (or her) to cope with successfully.[21]

The main features of this are utilitarianism, the greatest good for the greatest number, and the notion of testing in the service of the community, helping to ensure that the best use is made of all talent in the schools. The relationship between testing and the community was in fact one of Thomson's main concerns, and his position was unequivocal:

> ... how many educated intelligences does a modern community need? Now for my own part I reply to this without hesitation with the answer, as many as it can possibly get.[22]

Indeed it is only a slight exaggeration to say that he saw intelligence as being necessary and sufficient for civilisation, since he asserted that 'the history of the advance of civilisation has been the history of the conquest of the world by intelligence'[23] and that 'intelligence, education and law-abiding go together, all three'.[24] Yet despite the central importance with which he endowed intelligence, he did not see it as a virtue:

> To say that a child is intelligent is not a compliment, it is a description. The child cannot help being intelligent ... and deserves no more credit for it than for his blue eyes or his snub nose. He deserves credit or discredit, I think, for his use of misuse of his intelligence.[25]

For Thomson, then, intelligence was an attribute of the individual like height or eye colour, but one whose accurate identification and efficient exploitation were in the best interests of the community. An important goal, therefore, of education was to sieve out various levels of intelligence and provide them with the appropriate amount and type of training. This approach emphasises differences in kinds of ability just as much as differences in amount and is the natural opinion to be expected from one who thought about intelligence as Thomson did.

The educational structure which he advocated as the best way of achieving this 'sieve' effect also reflected these features. Physiological changes caused by the onset of puberty have such far-reaching educational implications 'that there should be a definite break in school-life at about the age of eleven plus'.[26] After this break, the 'nursery-like atmosphere of the primary school (is) no longer suitable'[27] and should be replaced by 'an atmosphere of greater responsibility, and more an air of looking to the outer world and the life-work'.[28] Since 'for the adolescent, decidedly different kinds of treatment are imperative'[29] some educational streaming would have to be incorporated. Thomson advocated a continuation of a 'kind of academic curriculum which leads up to .... the universities and the professions'[30] but proposed as a second major educational track a curriculum which

> must provide for training in morals and citizenship, for Music and for Physical Exercises, as well as for ... the English subjects, together with Mathematics and Science and, as a rule, Drawing ... aptitudes of individual scholars may be catered for, by courses in practical subjects such as Benchwork, Dairying or Cookery, by Commercial subjects or by a foreign language.[31]

In short, apart from the academic stress of the former curriculum, Thomson also advocated 'a course which may range from one which is definitely vocational to one which is not distinguishable from the course in secondary schools which we have decided to call grammar schools'.[32]

The type of segregation implied in these recommendations lays as much emphasis on catering for different types of ability as on different levels. Thomson was aware of the social implications of this distinction, writing that, if segregation were based solely on general intelligence, 'it would be almost, probably quite, impossible, to prevent social distinctions accompanying the distinction of type of mind.[33] On the other hand, Thomson's view that educational segregation should not involve a value judgement, along with his refusal to see intelligence as a virtue, led him to conclude that the aim of selection should be 'to create the different types of school side by side in a social equality, without permitting them to appear higher or lower in a scale of snobbishness'.[34]

However, a comparison of these features with the arrangements for education after age eleven which operated in Britain between the wars indicates that the aims of the latter, and hence the role played by testing, differed greatly from those suggested by Thomson. The comparison is complicated by two circumstances; first, the existence of separate educational codes which operated respectively in Scotland and in England and Wales; and secondly, the fact that, as Robertson remarks, 'in the last twenty-five years of his life, (1930-55) Thomson rarely wrote or spoke (outside the classroom) on general education subjects'[35] and that in particular, his major work on education, to which most of the notes in the preceding few paragraphs refer, was never revised after its publication in 1929.

The existence of an independent educational administration in Scotland is of course a legacy of the fact that, for most of its history, Scotland has been independent of England. However, although the administrative details differed widely and a different terminology was used, the problems besetting the concepts of testing and educational selection had much in common and the fate of attempts to overcome them was much the same. In England and Wales, the free place examination, instituted in 1907, was intended not to be a qualifying examination but merely to ensure that the introduction of free places ' ... shall not have the effect of lowering the standard of education provided by the school'.[36] By 1936, however, the idea of not regarding it as a qualifier had been dropped and it was admitted that ' ... the purpose of the examination is the selection ... of children fit to profit by secondary education ... the main business is to get the right children'.[37] Similarly, in Scotland, the centrally-set qualifying examination at age 12, which had previously been the responsibility of the Scottish Education Department in London, was abolished in 1923 to be replaced by local 'control examinations' set by County Education Authorities which had been set up in Scotland by an Act of 1918. The standard work on the history of education in Scotland remarks that 'undoubtedly the attempt was to get rid of the concept of "qualifying"' but goes on to note that:

> a distinction was retained nevertheless between 'junior secondary' (for those failing the examination) of three and 'senior' (for those passing it) of five years and this was a crucial point since it fostered jealousy, frustration, pressure, disappointment and strain, if not among pupils, at least among many parents.[38]

Inevitably,

> If performance in the test determined, as it did, whether a pupil went to a secondary, intermediate or an 'advanced division' (virtually non-secondary) course, there was a demand by parents which conscientious teachers found hard to resist for meticulous preparation directly aimed at the examination.[39]

Under both codes, then, at attempt was made to abolish the concept of qualification and under both codes, the attempt <u>de facto</u> failed. The substitution of 'promotion' or 'control' for 'qualifying' examination schemes did not prevent the education provided for children successful therein being described as 'the only truly secondary education'.[40] Therefore the attempt to introduce parallel ladders for different types of intellect, which if successful would have brought the school system much closer to that advocated by Thomson, did not succeed and the effects of selection continued to be socially divisive in the very sense which, as we have seen, Thomson felt should be avoided. In Scotland (which if anything made greater attempts to combat the problem than England) less than 20% of primary schools in the 1920s with advanced divisions[41] offered courses leading to the Higher Day School Certificate which 'possessed some standing'[42] and only about one child in six reached the third and final year of this certificate.[43] In Scotland, therefore, as in England, those children failing the critical examination (whatever it was called) largely ended up simply waiting for the school leaving age of 14, and the practical effect of the examination was to constitute an 'asses' bridge' (by which name it was popularly known in Scotland) of exactly the sort Thomson deprecated.

The first complication mentioned above then - the separate codes for England and Wales and for Scotland - makes little difference as far as the present paper is concerned, and enough has been said on this point since it is not the purpose at present to explore these discrepancies _per se_. The second complication, however, the lack of writings on education in Thomson's publications after 1930, does make things rather more difficult.

It has already been remarked that Thomson viewed with approval the _intended_ type of education to be provided in Scotland after age twelve for children who did not do well in the 'promotion' examination. Even the Lower Day School Certificate, taken at age 14 and intended as the minimum educational qualification for any child, was 'designed to continue and develop the pupil's general education, not only in the intellectual but also in the moral and physical spheres and at the same time to include a practical element with a broad vocational bias'[44] - very much as Thomson recommended.

Moreover, he was not alone in regarding the syllabus approvingly and optimistically. Writing in 1927, twelve months before Thomson and four years after the introduction of the Day School Certificates for those failing the 'promotion' examination, Alexander Morgan wrote that the courses

> staffed by carefully selected and thoroughly qualified teachers, should make the education given in the last two or three important years in the primary school more successful than ever before.[45]

There appears to have been a general air of optimism among educationists that the new courses would genuinely solve the problem of bipartite education after age twelve.

The historian's view, unfortunately, is rather different. The advanced divisions:

> came in for much criticism almost throughout their existence. The standard of work done was generally held to be poor, inferior to secondary schooling in content, premises and equipment, and certainly not regarded as equivalent by industrial and business concerns. One great weakness of the courses was the lack of trained staff ...[46]

So much for 'carefully selected and thoroughly qualified teachers'. These courses, offered in the higher years of primary schools, corresponding to the 'higher tops' in England, were undoubtedly a disappointment; and if this is particularly so in Scotland, it is probably not because they were worse than elsewhere but because more was initially expected of them.

The present discussion is based entirely on published sources and in view of this, it should now be clear why the lack of references to educational administration in Thomson's published work after 1929 is so much of a problem. His last detailed writings in this area appeared at a time when it was still reasonable to hope that the role of the test in the educational system was, at least in Scotland, tolerably consonant with that which he recommended. His writings after that do not record his reaction to an inevitably growing realisation that this hope was not being fulfilled. In 1954, the year before his death, he wrote to the third impression of his 1929 book that

> there are ... expressions of opinion not in accordance with my present views. But with the general tenor of the whole I am still in agreement[47].

Such ambiguity is hardly informative. It is possible that unpublished material may in the future throw light on Thomson's reaction to this conflict between psychological theory and educational policy, and the examination of unpublished papers is clearly an important priority for research in this field. On present evidence, however, it is not possible to infer anything more than the global point that whatever Thomson saw as the disadvantages of testing, he felt that they were outweighed by the benefits to be gained from it. This is indicated by the fact that he continued to produce tests into the 1940s, by which time the Scottish educational arrangements, on which such hopes had been placed, had been operative for twenty years.

The question to which this paper is addressed was asked previously in a rather more direct way (and, significantly perhaps, not answered), by P. E. Vernon, himself a prominent student of psychometrics, who asked, of the eleven-plus examination,

> Was he (Godfrey Thomson) more proud of the tremendous technical achievement, or regretful of the public controversies and misunderstandings, the parental neuroses, and the distortions of primary teaching to which it led?[48]

To this, Robertson replied,

> The eleven-plus would have been with us just the same, even if Binet and Terman, Burt and Thomson, had never lived. It was the creation not of the testers but of the Acts of 1944/45, the shortage of selective-school places, the new affluence of the working classes, and the demand for grammar school education both as status-symbol and as career-asset. Only it would have been a worse kind of eleven-plus, with old-style tests of attainment as its chief selective instrument, thus aggravating all the ill-effects of which Vernon writes.[49]

Robertson's point may be valid enough, but it does not answer one question. Neither does the following comment from Sir Cyril Burt, who wrote in 1957 that

> Thomson has at times been criticised for an alleged inconsistency in that he apparently denies the existence of a general factor, and yet constructs numerous tests for what other writers would call general intelligence.

> And certainly at first sight it sounds as though his sampling theory was seeking to substitute a theory of unlimited small factors for a theory of one large factor. Yet from a neurological standpoint the net result is really the same. If the mind is a mass of neural units which show no differentiation among themselves, then those units are of the same type or quality throughout: in other words, there is a general factor, namely, the quality common to all. And on this basis Thomson's construction of intelligence tests seems fully justified.[50]

The determination with which Thomson opposed Spearman's notion of general ability makes it unlikely that he could have regarded his view and Spearman's as being 'really the same'.

In contrast, the aim of the present paper has been to illustrate an incongruity between two strands of Thomson's work and to trace its root to the effects of policy constraints, i.e. to argue that tensions between Thomson's views on the nature of intelligence and the type of test he devised can best be explained by looking at his awareness of such constraints. Unfortunately, as noted above, the period during which these tensions can most usefully be studied was the period when his publications made least reference to the effect of educational administration, thus throwing even greater emphasis on unpublished sources.

One conclusion which can be drawn from the above discussion, however, is that as an educationist - specifically as one of the first major advocates of what is now called comprehensive education - Thomson was ahead of his time. Indeed, he was too far ahead for there to be any indication during his lifetime that his proposals would become accepted at government level, an event which ahppened only some ten years after his death. Educational thought had to move a long way to reach Thomson's position and it is interesting that on the way, it moved into the system of selective education enshrined in the Education Acts of 1944/45 and associated with the name of Sir Cyril Burt, and then moved out of it again towards the comprehensive arrangement which began to be favoured in the later 1960s. To this extent, it is ironical that Thomson died in 1955 while Burt survived until 1971, for it means that each of them died when the other's educational ideas were in the ascendant - Thomson did not live to see his proposals implemented while Burt lived to see his being withdrawn.

The problem facing Thomson, then, was essentially that while his educational philosophy was free to be considerably ahead of his time, his contribution to testing as a part of selection was not, and the latter as a result had consequences other than those which he envisaged. It is a problem which may arise whenever work of considerable applied potential is being used in a context over which the originator has no control (though it does not necessarily arise under such circumstances - had it been Spearman rather than Thomson constructing the tests, there is no reason to suppose that there would have been any conflict of the type discussed here, despite the fact that Spearman would have had no more control than Thomson). This is certainly compatible with Paterson's view of Thomson's career as

> a good example of the dangers and delights of close links between educational theory and practice, and educational policy-making [51]

As someone who contributed significantly both to testing and to the theory of the intellect, Thomson probably illustrates better than anyone else the problems faced by social scientists concerning the application of their work. It is on these grounds that this aspect of his career is worthy of discussion.

REFERENCES

[1] See G. Sutherland, 'The magic of measurement: mental testing and English education 1900-1940', Transactions of the Royal Historical Society, 27, 1977, 135-153.

[2] For further details of this debate, see S. Sharp, 'Much ado about nothing: an evaluation of the Thomson-Spearman debate', unpublished manuscript, 1978.

[3] P. E. Vernon, 'The contributions to education of Sir Godfrey Thomson', British Journal for Educational Studies, 10, 1962, 123-137.

[4] J. J. Robertson, Godfrey Thomson, Moray House, Edinburgh. Fifth Godfrey Thomson Lecture, 1964.

[5] H. Paterson, 'Godfrey Thomson and the Development of Psychometrics in Scotland', paper read at the 1975 conference of the British Educational Research Association.

[6] R. E. Bell, 'Godfrey Thomson and Scottish Education', paper read at the 1975 conference of the British Educational Research Association.

[7] G. H. Thomson, The Education of an Englishman, Moray House, Edinburgh, 1969.

[8] The Long Vacation of 1911.

[9] B. Norton, 'Charles Spearman and the General Factor in intelligence: Genesis and Interpretation in the Light of Socio-personal Considerations', Journal for the History of the Behavioural Sciences, 15, 1979, 142-154.

[10] Ibid., 144-5, for more details. In modern terminology, the prediction is that the correlation matrix of a test battery has rank one.

[11] For example, C. Spearman, 'General intelligence objectively determined and measured', American Journal of Psychology, 15, 1904, 201-292, or B. Hart and C. Spearman, 'General ability, its existence and nature', British Journal of Psychology, 5, 1912, 51-84.

[12] G. H. Thomson, 'A Hierarchy without a general factor', British Journal of Psychology, 8, 1916, 271-281.

[13] Ibid., 281.

[14] G. H. Thomson, 'The hierarchy of abilities', British Journal of Psychology, 9, 1919, 337-344, 341. It would seem that if the notion of 'bonds' was suggested by anything, it was the dice, which played such a large part in Thomson's early arguments with Spearman.

[15] G. H. Thomson, The Factorial Analysis of Human Ability, London: University of London Press, 1951, 313. In this book, his main work on the topic, Thomson devoted only 21 of the 328 pages of the text to his own theory and the majority of these were given over to exploring the corresponding mathematical model, not to discussing the nature of 'bonds'.

[16] G. H. Thomson, 'Group factors in mental abilities', Psychological Review, 27, 1920, 173-190, 184.

[17] G. H. Thomson, 'Autobiography', in C. Murchison (ed.), History of Psychology in Autobiography, Worcester: Clark University Press, 1952, 279-294.

[18] Ibid., pp. 284-285.

[19] The debate was from 1916 until around the mid-1930s while the Moray House tests started in 1921 and are still in use today.

[20]It is true that, in addition to Moray House intelligence tests, Thomson also produced English and Arithmetic tests. But it is an open question as to whether this was due to his views on the nature of intelligence or as a result of pressure from local authorities who wished to adopt standardised, validated tests for secondary selection while avoiding too drastic a break from the previous methods and hence preferred tests which combined the new procedures with the old subject matter. The archive material which would permit a resolution to the matter does not seem to have survived.

[21]G. H. Thomson, What are Moray Houses Tests?, London University Press, 1940, p.3.

[22]G. H. Thomson, 'Intelligence and civilisation', Journal of the University of Manchester, 1, 1937, 18-38, p. 29.

[23]Ibid., pp. 31-32.

[24]Ibid., p. 37.

[25]G. H. Thomson, A Modern Philosophy of Education, London: Allen and Unwin, 1929, p. 272.

[26]Ibid., p. 199.

[27]Ibid., p. 215.

[28]Ibid., p. 215.

[29]Ibid., p. 271.

[30]Ibid., p. 210.

[31]Ibid., p. 210. Thomson here is quoting the provisions laid down by the Scottish Education Department for the Scottish Advanced Divisions (see below note 41) but does so approvingly and clearly favoured the introduction of such a scheme of study.

[32]Ibid., p. 210.

[33]Ibid., p. 272.

[34]Ibid., p. 271.

[35]J. J. Robertson, op. cit., p. 13.

[36]Annual Report of the Board of Education 1906-7, p. 67, quoted by G. Sutherland, op. cit., p. 144.

[37]Special Place Examinations, Board of Education Pamphlet, London, 1936, p. 4, quoted in G. Sutherland, op. cit., p. 147.

[38]J. Scotland, The History of Scottish Education, Vol. II, London: University of London Press, 1969, p. 73.

[39]Ibid., p. 59.

[40]I. R. Findlay, Education in Scotland, Newton Abbott: David & Charles, 1973, p.30.

[41]J. Scotland, op. cit., p. 73. The advanced divisions catered for children failing the 'promotion' examination and led to the Day School Certificate, either Higher (after three) or Lower (after two) years. The former obviously carried more prestige but was still far enough behind the full five-year secondary course to foster the jealousy, etc., referred to in quotation 38 above.

[42]Ibid., p. 73.

[43]S. L. Hunter, The Scottish Educational System, second edition, Oxford: Pergamon Press, 1971, p. 13.

[44] H. M. Knox, Two Hundred and Fifty Years of Scottish Education, Edinburgh: Oliver and Boyd, 1953, p. 211.

[45] A. Morgan, The Rise and Progress of Scottish Education, Edinburgh: Oliver and Boyd, 1927, p. 202.

[46] J. Scotland, op. cit., p. 58.

[47] G. H. Thomson, A Modern Philosophy of Education, op. cit., postcript to the third impression, 1954, p. 8.

[48] P. E. Vernon, op. cit., p. 137.

[49] J. J. Robertson, op. cit. p. 7. Robertson, however. begs the question to some extent by ignoring the possibility that Thomson's contribution was crucial to the establishment of testing as an activity on which an Act could be partly based and that hence without him, the Acts might never have been passed.

[50] C. L. Burt, The Application of Mathematics to Psychology, Moray House, Edinburgh. First Godfrey Thomson Lecture, 1957.

[51] H. Paterson, op. cit., p. 18.

ACKNOWLEDGEMENT

Thanks are due to Gillian Sutherland and David Hamilton for helpful comments on various drafts of this paper.

MEASURING INTELLIGENCE: ENGLISH LOCAL EDUCATION AUTHORITIES AND MENTAL TESTING 1919-1939

Gillian Sutherland
Fellow of Newnham College
University of Cambridge

ABSTRACT

This paper examines aspects of the reception accorded, in England, to the new technology of mental measurement, in the period between the two World Wars. It focuses not on the academic discussion but on the recognition this received and the resonances it evoked among those who actually ran the schools in the period, the teachers, the local authority members and their officers. It includes some account of the use of this technology and a discussion of an explanatory framework for the peculiarities of this.

****

Alexander Bain's Education as a Science was Vol. 25 in Kegan Paul's International Scientific Series, preceded by such volumes as R. H. Thurston's A History of the Growth of the Steam Engine and Norman Lockyer's Studies in Spectrum Analysis; but also by Herbert Spencer's The Study of Sociology and Bagehot's Physics and Politics. In Chapter V, ' Education Values', Bain wrote

> Of Science generally we can remark, first, that it is the most perfect embodiment of Truth and of the ways of getting at Truth. More than anything else does it impress the mind with the nature of Evidence, with the labour and precautions necessary to prove a thing. It is the gran corrective of the laxness of the natural man in receiving unaccredited facts and conclusions.[1]

And the whole book is intended to show how education can be approached in this way - a 'war', as he says, 'not so much against error as against confusion'.[2] The appeal to science as the embodiment of certainty, the insistence that his particular specialism conforms to a model derived from the 'hardest' physical science, is too familiar a phenomenon among nineteenth- and twentieth-century social scientists to need more elaboration here. The new specialism of the psychology of individual differences, emerging from the turn of the century, was no exception to this, nor was its principal field of application, education. The proponents of mental measurement, or psychometrics, as some of them chose to call it, offered it to teachers and educational administrators as the new technology which would at last enable the theory and practice of education to attain scientific status.[3] The Scottish and American experiences encourage one to expect teachers, politicians and administrators to take the technology of mental measurement very seriously indeed. The Scottish Council for Research into Education was established in 1930 and the first Scottish National Survey was carried out in 1932. Clarence Karier has written of the 'quasi-public bureaucracy of boards, compacts, councils and Commissions which serve to shape policy by giving and withholding both public and private funds at key points in the (American educational) system',[4] and he instances, in particular, the American Council on Education, the Carnegie Foundation and the creation of the Educational Testing Service.

The two obvious areas of applicability for the new technology in England were first, the identification of the subnormal and second, the classification of the normal. Individual Binet tests were already in use in England for the identification of mentally defective children by the outbreak of the First World War. This forms a relatively self-contained subject for investigation, which I have discussed elsewhere.[5] Classification of the normal may mean simply 'tracking' or 'streaming' within the school. Alternatively, or in addition, it may mean the segregation of children into different schools at given ages. Such segregation was taking place in English education in the first half of the twentieth century. Between the ages of ten and twelve a tiny minority of children were chosen to proceed to secondary schools, where they could stay until the age of eighteen; the majority remained in elementary schools, which they left at fourteen. This process of choice is the obvious place at which to start looking for the large-scale impact of the new technology in England. And indeed, the standard text, Olive Banks' Parity and Prestige in English Secondary Education, declares that

> By the outbreak of War in 1939 the use of intelligence tests and standardized tests of English and Arithmetic with appropriate age allowances had been adopted by almost every local authority in an attempt to ensure that maximum efficiency in the selection of children for the places available.[6]

She gives no source for this statement and it is simply not true. Only 68 out of the 128 Local Education Authorities with responsibility for secondary education in England are now known to have used some type of group intelligence test, for some purpose in secondary selection, at some point between 1919 and 1940.[7] That is to say, only just over half of them used something they called an intelligence test - and perhaps only once - in what came to be known as the '11+' examination. Far fewer used standardized English and Arithmetic tests. Indeed, the use of these seems to have been primarily a function of the decision to use Moray House intelligence tests and the subsequent discovery that, conveniently, Moray House provided English and Arithmetic tests as well; and I don't propose to discuss these any further now. The symbol of the new technology was the group intelligence or mental test - the terms were used interchangeably in this period; and it seems the English were markedly less enthusiastic about it than either the Americans or the Scots.[8]

How to begin to explain the peculiarities of the English? There is space to present only part of the discussion now.[9] I shall concentrate here on the personnel involved in taking the crucial decisions, the information about testing to which they had access, their attitudes and the social and political structures they represent. These, of course, interact and reinforce each other and any attempt to disentangle them must be an artificial device, purely for explanatory purposes. The process is further complicated by the fact that although there was a national debate, the effective decisions were taken at a local level.

It is important to be clear at the outset that the English educational public was not notably ill-informed about the notion of intelligence and its attendant, burgeoning technology. Cyril Burt claimed that the term 'intelligence' in its modern sense was first used by Herbert Spencer. But Keith Hope has shown its wide currency during the nineteenth century, stretching back at least to writers of the Scottish Enlightenment at the end of the eighteenth century.[10] As early as 1913 The Times Educational Supplement reported that Surrey County Council was conducting a secondary school selection examination, in the final oral examination of which 'the candidates are marked for general intelligence'.[11] By the mid 1920s, 'general intelligence' was as much a part of the stock-in-trade of public discussion as, say, 'national efficiency' had been twenty years earlier. In June 1926 the President, Alderman George Cadbury, explained to the Annual Conference of the Association for Education in Industry and Commerce the problems of balancing quantitative and qualitative considerations in chocolate making, and he summed up, 'general intelligence is of the utmost value in promoting efficiency'.[12] In June 1927 an advertisement for the Singer Sewing Machine in the weekly journal Education quoted an un-named headmistress as declaring 'The Needlework Lesson now seems to develop general intelligence, too!'[13]

This kind of cant use was hardly technically precise. But use of a word or catch-phrase like this usually follows on from a more technically informed discussion and this case was no exception. The educational journals regularly reviewed books and reported discussions on intelligence and mental measurement. In 1919, 'in response to a number of inquiries', The Times Educational Supplement provided a reading list on the subject. In 1920 they gave a very long and careful review to Burt's The Distribution of Mental Abilities. The following year they reviewed recent American group tests, pointing out that many of them were really attainment tests.[14]

Perhaps typical of the many lengthily reported conference discussions was the session on 'Psychological Tests' at the Imperial Education Conference in 1927, at which

> Dr Ballard said that too often 'intelligent' means 'interested in the things that interest me'. The psychologist applies a different interpretation: to him intelligence is independent of training, of knowledge, of culture, even of interest. He is looking, not for performance but for promise. The usual verbal tests need to be supplemented by other tests in order to test intelligence in the true psychological sense.[15]

Ballard matched Burt as one of the most popular, or, at least, most frequently heard, lecturers on the rationale and technology of testing.[16] But the professionals in general seem to have devoted considerable time and energy to the work of propaganda. In 1919, with great public fanfare, the British Psychological Society opened its meetings to practising teachers, no longer confining them to accredited research workers.[17] By 1926 the National Institute of Industrial Psychology was advertising a set of five lecture-demonstrations for teachers on intelligence tests, which could be hired by any Local Education Authority in the country.[18]

The debate and discussion was not all one-sided. Ballard's colleague in the London County Council inspectorate, F. H. Hayward, the licensed clown of the educational world in the early 1920s, barracked constantly from the side-lines, stigmatizing intelligence tests as merely 'tests of cleverness'.[19] Others, such as Professor John Adams of University College, London, Professor J. A. Green of Sheffield, Frank Watts, Lecturer in Psychology at Manchester, Professor T. H. Pear of Manchester and Professor E. H. Campagnac of Liverpool, took and developed more seriously Hayward's basic point, the difficulty of separating intelligence from the universe in which it had to operate, the problems with which it had to deal. They discussed questions of motivation, of particular aptitudes and the whole issue of culture loading.[20]

I have discussed briefly elsewhere the contribution of the Board of Education and its inspectorate to this discussion and said a little also about the impotence of the central authority in this period.[21] The Local Education Authorities, as both sides were aware, called the tune. One of the principal motives in the planning for post-Second-World-War reconstruction begun by the higher officials of the Board of Education as early as November 1940, was the wish to regain the initiative from the LEAs.[22] To understand the response in English schools between the Wars to the kind of discussion outlined above, we have to look in detail at these local authorities and their employees, both officials and teachers, and prepare ourselves in advance for considerable diversity and the likelihood of no tidy patterning. We can make the transition from national to local most easily if we start looking not just at discussions of intelligence and mental testing, but at discussions of examinations and notions of measurement more generally. Measurement was, in certain crucial senses, still a dirty word in English education. It was so because of payment by results, the system whereby from 1863 to 1890 the bulk of the government grant to a school (almost half its income) depended upon the performance of each child, each year in examinations, written and oral, conducted by Her Majesty's Inspectors.[23] The habits engendered by this Procrustean system lasted longer than the system itself; and indeed there were still teachers in the schools in the 1920s who had trained and begun to teach under it. The battle against payment by results had been the National Union of Teachers' first big battle and their eventual emancipation from its trammels was regarded as a crucial stage in the fight for professional status.[24]

But the efficiency of any mechanism of competitive examination depends to a considerable extent on having a sufficiently large and representative population of examinees. Thus the Northumberland Education Committee had decreed that all the children of the appropriate age group should be examined by Godfrey Thomson in 1921.[25] By 1924 the Middlesex Education Committee had determined to subject all its elementary schools to what were called 'efficiency tests', 'designed to determine the number of their pupils likely to profit by a secondary school course'.[26] They were promptly denounced by the NUT, whose conference in 1925 deplored any 'reversion to the individual examination system' and protested 'emphatically against the tendency observable in some areas to use the examination for scholarships to secondary schools as a test of the efficiency of primary schools, instead of what it should be - a test of the child's natural ability'.[27] The Association of Education Committees, the LEA trade union, added fuel to the flames by defending the rights of its member authorities to assess the efficiency of the schools for which they were responsible. Indeed, they encouraged them to do so and a major slanging match ensued.[28] Eventually both sides nominated representatives to a specially formed committee, which then spent nearly four years producing a report so qualified and anodyne as to make no impact at all.[29]

Mass examinations were thus an extremely sensitive subject in elementary schools in the inter-war period. I have discussed elsewhere the possible challenge posed by group intelligence tests in particular to these teachers' hard-won but still precarious social and intellectual authority.[30] The net effect was to make the reactions of elementary school teachers to any such proposals very unpredictable indeed. Nationally the NUT kept a very low profile on intelligence tests and its own Examining Board, significantly, never attempted to experiment with them.[31] Locally, the reaction might depend very much on whose idea it was and how diplomatically it was done. For example, while the teachers in the Isle of Wight seem to have co-operated fully in some very sophisticated uses of Moray House Tests throughout the 1930s,[32] those in the North Riding of Yorkshire were up in arms in 1931 about the 'intelligence test' paper sprung on them in that year's Junior Scholarship Examination.[33] In Leicestershire, one of the earliest users of group intelligence tests, W. R. Brockington, the Director of Education worried continually about teachers coaching for them.[34]

The teachers in the elementary schools were not, of course, the only teachers upon whom selective examinations for secondary schools impinged. There were also the secondary school teachers. One's first thought is that they surely had everything to gain by an 'efficient' selection process. Certainly they did not share the collective sensitivity of the elementary school teachers about the examination process; and some, indeed, took to the new technology in an enthusiastic and well-informed way. In 1922, at the request of the Sunderland County Borough Council Higher Education Sub-Committee, the head teachers of the Bede Collegiate Schools prepared a most lucid and well-illustrated report, beginning 'Intelligence Tests are an attempt to measure intellectual ability apart from scholastic attainment. The questions must therefore require thought and ordinary general knowledge but no special knowledge'.[35]

After trials and consultation with HM Inspectorate, they were by 1927 using a standard group test - the Otis - as a check upon the English and arithmetic marks in the selection examination; that is to say, they did not lump the test score in with the rest, but compared it with the total mark for the attainments tests and followed up any major discrepancies.[36] In Halifax secondary and elementary heads seem to have made the pace between 1927 and 1936 in bringing about a selection system dependent primarily upon group intelligence tests (Moray House) and standardized elementary school record cards. HM Inspectors found themselves in the somewhat unusual position of having to reassure members of the Education Committee that this was a good system.[37]

But examples like these are somewhat exceptional. Far more often mention of a test of 'general intelligence' in the selection process turns out, on further investigation, to mean that there is an interview or oral examination conducted by one or more secondary head teachers at which questions either made up by them or chosen at random from some of the better known group tests are asked.[38] Handled skilfully and systematically, such interviews might approach the rigour of an individual Binet. But there is an instructive correspondence in The Times Educational Supplement in 1921, started by 'Secondary Headmaster' who wrote as follows:

> To each of thirty-five candidates, the most highly recommended out of ninety, from the elementary schools of my neighbourhood I gave as an oral test in a free place examination last week this question which they read in print from a paper:-
>
> > 'Captain Cook made three voyages to the South Seas. On one of these voyages he was killed. On which one?'
>
> Only six of the thirty-five candidates could answer this question correctly. The candidates were aged between ten and twelve years. Which is wrong - the test or the intelligence of the children?[39]

The majority of the heads among his respondents took him perfectly seriously; and it was left to the indefatigable Ballard to try to explain that proper intelligence test were not conducted like that.[40]

There is a television quiz game element in this kind of thing which one hopes the poor victims were not too terrified to appreciate. But such interviews were surely intended also to demonstrate and enhance the authority of the interviewer. The rationale of playing God like this was set out at its grandest in a paper read by J. L. Paton, High Master of Manchester Grammar School, to the North of England Education Conference in 1920. He considered the extended interviews he conducted infinitely superior to any intelligence test, describing types of questions which ranged from asking for a summary of passages from Addison and Macaulay to sums about the accommodation of motor cars in garages. He ended

> While you are discussing this ... and whatever may arise out of it, you are gauging from that boy's replies, and specially from the way he speaks and the set of his lips, what his will-power is. This is, perhaps, the most important thing of all. What has this boy set himself to be? That more than anything else will determine his future ... This is where Simon-Binet fails us. Your boy may have a first-rate capacity for knowledge, but all he may want to know is all about the Carpentier-Beckett fight. The all-important thing about him is what sort of knowledge does he hunger for? And is his desire for it steadfast? Is it what economists call 'effective demand'? Will it be strong enough to resist the infections of the street with its posters and its newspaper placards? Will he have a soul that refuses to be fed on these things? Will he know the higher from the lower? The temporary from the abiding? And will he choose the better and eschew the worse? Has he his soul, as Plato would say, turned towards the light? If so, he is the lad your school was meant to help and he will help it as much as it helps him.[41]

Thus the final selection of the _crème de la crème_ from Manchester Grammar School. But secondary school heads throughout the country clung on hard to any and all discretions given them in the selection process.[42] Part of this is explicable in terms of a whole framework of belief, not confined to secondary school heads, to which I shall return below. But some of it seems rooted in a peculiar combination and interaction of two factors, the graduate status of secondary school heads and the buyer's market in which they operated. Their graduate status distanced them from the lowly elementary school teacher, even college-trained, and placed them within the ranks of the local professional elite. But it also meant that their formal training in education was _nil_. They were much less likely than elementary school teachers to have a sustained and formal encounter with considerations of teaching and examining techniques and of mental and psychological testing as it, too, found its way into training college curricula.[43] By a buyer's market I mean that competition for places was such that secondary school headmasters could usually pick and choose. In the selection process, particularly if it included an interview, was a considerable amount of patronage, the exercise of which some of them plainly enjoyed.

The remaining occupational group heavily involved with secondary school selection were the local education officials. Again, one's first thought is that the attraction of the new examination technology, with all its claims to objectivity and precision must have been powerful. Yet again, the reality was more complex and reactions much more mixed. Their occupation had, effectively, been created by the Education Act of 1902 when it created authorities large enough to need full-time professional administrative support. They promptly formed not one but two professional associations; but by 1919 had managed to amalgamate them.[44] By the end of 1937 they had secured the agreement of the AEC and the County Councils Association to a standard job definition and terms of service.[45]

But the terms of this job description reflected perfectly some continuing tensions within the formal grouping. It declared,

> administrative ability and experience are essential while technical knowledge, such as can best be acquired by actual teaching experience in some type or types of school is very desirable. Such officers should, of course, have received a sound general education and the possession of a good university degree is most expedient.[46]

The Association of Directors and Secretaries of Education contained two distinct groups: on the one hand, the older breed of lower-middle class, upwardly socially mobile ex-elementary school teachers, ex-NUT officials, ex-school board clerks, if graduates, mature students and often London external students; on the other, slightly younger middle class graduates of the more conventional kind, with perhaps some token years of teaching experience, who, fifty years earlier, might have become public schoolmasters, briefless barristers, or even, immediately after 1870, HM Inspectors of Schools.[47] Among the former could be counted Thomas Walling at Newcastle-upon-Tyne, Spurley Hey at Manchester, Thomas Boyce at Bradford, Percival Sharp at Sheffield and A. R. Pickles at Burnley.[48] Among the latter were Salter Davies in Kent, Keith Innes in Wiltshire, W. R. Brockington in Leicestershire, G. H. Gater in Lancashire and then at the L.C.C. and, by election, Henry Morris in Cambridgeshire.

This second group - career local civil servants, if you like - included some of the earliest and most committed exponents of mental testing, notably Brockington and Salter Davies; and the introduction of testing in Wiltshire seems to have coincided with Innes' arrival.[50]

Pickles, on the other hand, provides an exceptionally interesting example of the reactions of an experienced ex-teacher to the new technology. Some of it he found acceptable, some not. At the North of England Conference on Education in 1931, he discussed at length the theory about the relationship between general and specific abilities, concluding, 'it is therefore likely that selection for further education at the age of eleven will remain based on range of central capacity rather than type of special ability'. Then he went on,

> There is great scope for experiment and research into the methods of transfer from junior schools. No course of senior grade can be properly planned without knowledge of the basis of attainment and capacity reached in the fundamental subjects of the curriculum, and the question of what the normal pupil can or cannot be expected to do assumes a new significance. It will be necessary to know what a pupil can actually do as well as what he is capable of doing. As internal examinations are 'tightened up' the school record will become increasingly valuable; but some form and measure of standardisation will still be desirable. Intelligence tests are still on their trial. Whilst attainment may possibly be tested apart from capacity, it is certain that capacity cannot be ascertained apart from attainment. It is yet doubtful whether intelligence tests measure real capacity; they rather tend to show up sharpness and quickness of reaction, to be by way of puzzles rather than problems. 'If your grandfather's only child was your uncle, draw a square, if not draw a circle.' Whilst there may be a permanent place for intelligence tests in the educational scheme, it is probable that a good examination can test intelligence

> and capacity quite as well as these artificial aids. But the sponsors of intelligence tests are undoubtedly showing how examinations can be reformed.[51]

His authority, Burnley, appears to have flirted only once - in March 1922 - with a group test.[52] But the fit is not perfect. The ex-elementary teachers Walling and Boyce, at Newcastle-upon-Tyne and Bradford respectively, presided over selection systems where mental testing was used.[53] By contrast, the London County Council did not use mental testing in the Junior County Scholarship Examination either in the time of Gater, or that of his successor, Edmund Rich.[54] Once again, the tidy pattern eludes us.

The last group involved with selection for secondary education is the one which it is most difficult to characterize, and yet the one which made the decisions - the councillors and aldermen who sat on the Education Committees. At the simplest level, they are difficult to characterize because they share no occupational description. However committed and informed they might become about their chosen specialism, their local government work remained ultimately voluntary and part-time. These difficulties are compounded by major problems of evidence. Anyone who has worked on twentieth-century local government records will know how frighteningly incomplete and uninformative they mostly are. Thus it is difficult enough to discover the grounds given for something new, e.g. the decision to try an intelligence test. By definition, hardly anyone bothers to explain carrying on as before. It is, however, possible to say a little about the general social standing of these people. County and county borough councillors and aldermen were firmly part of the local elite. The reform of English local government at the end of the nineteenth century had brought about no social revolution. The county councils, at least up to 1974, remained remarkably aristocratic bodies. In industrial and the more heavily urbanized areas business and professional men gradually elbowed out the old squirearchy, but without necessarily bringing much change of style.[55] Among the most prominent and active members of the Association of Education Committees in the inter-war years were men like the substantial textile manufacturer Alderman Sir Percy Jackson, Chairman of the West Riding Education Committee from 1917 to 1937, the local solicitor, Alderman Lieutenant-Colonel W. E. Raley, Chairman of the Barnsley Education Committee from 1904 to the end of the 1920s and Councillor W. Byng Kenrick, nephew of Joseph Chamberlain and director of the family hardware firm, who succeeded another uncle as Chairman of the Birmingham Education Committee in 1921.[56] Among this company, even the self-made men are rare and I have so far identified only two, Alderman E. G. Rowlinson, the railway trade union official, Chairman of the Sheffield Education Committee from 1926,[57] and George Tomlinson, the Lancashire weaver and union official, a member of the Lancashire Education Committee from 1930[58] and of course to succeed Ellen Wilkinson as Minister of Education in the Labour Government in 1947.

Rowlinson, like Tomlinson, was a solid Labour man. But there has emerged no simple or necessary correlation between progressive politics - or, indeed, any other sort - and a predilection for the new technology in education. Rowlinson's fellow-alderman from Sheffield, H. W. Jackson, indeed embarrassed him badly when he launched a thorough-going attack on psychologists in general and child guidance clinics in particular at the AEC meetings in 1938 and 1939.[59] One thinks again of the Halifax Education Committee seeking reassurance from HM Inspectorate that the system of selection was a good one.[60] But there were 'sports' if you like, testing enthusiasts among LEA members. It was Dr Andrew Messer who, single-handed, persuaded Northumberland to employ Godfrey Thomson in 1921.[61] The Bradford authority, for at least four years running, accepted advice and help from 'the Intelligence Tests Committee, an unofficial body of persons interested in such tests and willing to co-operate in investigating their possibilities in Bradford'[62] - about whom I would give a good deal to know more. And of course any Director or

Chief Education Officer worth his salt, the Brockingtons and Davieses, or indeed, the Wallings and Boyces, could carry his Committee with him at least part of the way when he wanted to do something very much.

This brings us full circle. If some officials, authorities - and teachers - considered intelligence tests the most 'efficient' way of selecting for secondary education, why did others not? I have tried to sketch the complexity of the social and political structure within which decisions were taken and through which information about the new technology was mediated. But to sum this up simply as vested interests and their rationalizations seems too crude - unless one is going to dismiss all ideas, all ideologies as epiphenomena of this kind. These networks of interests and the associated attitudes seem ultimately to require a broader frame of reference, some consideration of the role of educational selection in the society as a whole and a discussion of a notion of meritocracy which is peculiarly English.

Central to the concept of meritocracy is the equation of ability with merit, of talent with virtue, as Clarence Karier has called it.[63] This equation can be seen as a very tight, close relationship, possession of one guaranteeing and automatically bringing the other. On this interpretation, the related notion of equality of opportunity becomes quite a strong one, with at least an aura of democracy. But the English, from Macaulay and the Whig-Liberal reformers of the civil service onwards, have tended to see what is simultaneously a much looser and more complex relationship between the two. At the centre is a notion of merit which has social and cultural as well as more narrowly intellectual aspects; gradually, the possession of ability comes to be seen as _a_ principal, but not invariably _the_ principal, means of achieving this condition. Money, parental culture and aspiration may also make a contribution. It is perhaps hardly surprising to find this in a society with a class structure as well articulated as that of nineteenth-century England; and some members of that society recognized it clearly. The influential Royal Commission, the Taunton Commission, which reviewed the state of secondary education in the 1860s, presented the class stratification of English education as a _fait accompli_, which no act of policy could change. Type and duration of education were determined for the child by the finances and ambition of his parent. The Commissioners argued only for the re-modelling of old endowments to provide scholarships in order that 'real ability shall find its proper opening'.[64]

The dominant late nineteenth-century English version of meritocracy was thus both a weak and unashamedly socially elitist one. This is the context in which the first state-funded secondary schools were created after 1902. The ladder of scholarships of the kind recommended by the Taunton Commissioners, which linked public elementary schools to private and endowed secondary schools, had grown slowly since 1870. In 1907 the government made a first direct contribution to this. The Free Place Regulations of that year increased grants to secondary schools but made it a condition of the receipt of the full grant that a minimum of 25 per cent of the school's places should be free and open only to children from public elementary schools. The remainder of the schools' intake paid fees and could come from any preparatory school, public or private. _The Times Educational Supplement_, in one of its earliest issues in 1910, approved the principle but struck a warning note:

> to insist all at once upon so large a proportion as 25% of 'free-placers' _ex hypothesi_ boys or girls from working class homes, in an average secondary school to which middle class parents send their children, is, under present conditions of English life. to say the least of it, 'a large order' ... In an old country like England. where lines of social distinction are sharply drawn, they cannot be ignored or set aside in practice, however anxious we may be to open

> the best educational advantages to everyone. Most secondary school headmasters would welcome a contingent of capable working class boys to be absorbed into the life of the school and profit by its tone and teaching. But many of them are alarmed lest, if it be known or surmised that the numbers thus coming up from below are large enough to affect the tone and character of the school, the parents of paying pupils will hold aloof and the finances of the school become disorganized. Our administrators and reformers should be careful in the matter not to force the pace.[65]

This remains a theme well into the inter-war period. In 1925 Dr Terry Thomas, the new headmaster of Leeds Grammar School - who was to remain there until the middle 1950s - moved and carried at the Headmasters' Conference a resolution to the effect that a substantial extension of the free place system in existing schools would be unwise: 'They must be careful that their schools were not swamped. They had a great body of boys from middle class homes who might not be scholars but who were very valuable in building up a right tone in the school'.[66] This is the voice of social privilege. But the argument about 'tone' could and did transmute itself quite easily into an argument for high culture in the strictest Arnoldian sense. If you recall J. L. Paton's account of the interviews he gave to scholarship candidates for Manchester Grammar School, he laboured the distinction between a thirst for knowledge and the kind of knowledge sought. He wanted to discover the strength of a boy's determination and his motivation.[67]

Secondary school heads were, naturally enough, among the leading and most vocal exponents of this kind of highly structured elitism. But they were not the only ones. The economic crisis in 1931 led the government to propose the replacement of 'free places' by 'special places', entailing a means test to discover if the parent could pay part or even all of the fee. A handful of local authorities responded to this by declaring all their secondary school places special places and selecting for them by a uniform method; and this, indeed, was what the AEC Executive recommended.[68] But many more did not and continued to subject would-be fee-payers to a qualifying examination rather less stringent than the rigorous competition conducted for special places. Even those accepting the logic of a uniform method of selection were not necessarily convinced that a means test for fees was inegalitarian. When Alderman Rowlinson of Sheffield tried to move a resolution for free secondary education at the AEC annual conference in 1936, he got a somewhat warm reaction. Councillor W. M. Hyman (West Riding)

> deduced from the general argument by Alderman Rowlinson that the children of well-to-do-parents who could pay were in the main of lower intelligence than the children of those who required help with the fees. The parent without a bean should be able to produce the children of the highest intelligence and mental capacity!

On a card vote, the motion was lost by 248 to 181.[69]

It might have been expected that considerations of post-war economic reconstruction would have altered the terms of the debate somewhat. Certainly between 1915 and 1920 The Times Educational Supplement had declared at regular intervals that in future the nation could not afford to waste its 'child capital'.[70] But after 1920 statements of this kind largely disappeared. In so far as people adverted to the interests of the state in secondary education at all after 1920, they were as likely as not to suggest that the state was at risk from over-education. It was put very elegantly during the debate on the 1922 Education Estimates by Sir Martin

Conway, Conservative MP for the Combined English Universities:

> It is not, in fact, a ladder that we want from the lowest slum to the highest university honour, what we want is a sieve, so that we may be quite sure that not a grain is kept above the sieve that can get through it, and that not a grain large enough to remain in the top of the sieve gets lost. We want to sift the millions of children born in this country to discover, to isolate, to bring out, to help in every way, all the finest ability in the country, and allow none of it to escape. If you succeed in getting that, you really get all that is required, because the number of really able and most highly developed and educated people that are wanted will never be many.[71]

As economic depression deepened and unemployment increased, comments about the 'saturation' of professions and black-coated occupations became more explicit.[72]

In all the wrangling about special places the argument that ultimately the state would lose from the contraction of investment in education was heard only in a very weak form. Typical was the AEC Memorandum of 1932, which declared,

> It is desired - apart altogether from the enunciation of the simplest principles of justice - to emphasize that it is merely an elementary part of economic, social and political prudence to provide that the places in secondary schools maintained or aided by the nation should be allocated to children on an equal basis of merit. This is an ideal in secondary education which should not be forgone even in times of gravest national difficulty.[73]

When Alderman Rowlinson moved for free secondary education in 1936, he centred his argument not around national need but around the proposition 'that ability to take full advantage of higher education should be the criterion as to whether or not a child should go forward to this branch of education'.[74]

Thus in trying to explain why the reception given to the new technology of measurement in education in England in 1919 - 1939 was so lukewarm, we have first to recognize the decentralization of the decision-making process. Then we have to explore a complex social and political network, recognizing ultimately that we are dealing with a society whose educational system is highly and unashamedly elitist, whose version of meritocracy is a somewhat idiosyncratic one. We are dealing also with the society which was first to industrialize, from a relatively low educational base. This particular piece of historical experience made it extremely difficult for the English before the Second World War to perceive the force of the argument for spending on mass education as a form of investment for economic growth, thereby reinforcing the elitism.

****

The bulk of the work upon which this essay is based was funded by the Social Science Research Council and I am glad to acknowledge their generous support. In particular, their grant enabled Dr Stephen Sharp, now of the Godfrey Thomson Unit, University of Edinburgh, to work with me for two years and I am grateful for his help in collecting and analysing some of the data here discussed. A version of this essay is being published also in Biology, Medicine and Society 1840-1940 ed. Charles Webster for the Past and Present Society, by Cambridge University Press.

I am indebted to the Comptroller of Her Majesty's Stationery Office for permission to cite Crown Copyright material and to the librarians, archivists and other officers of The National Union of Teachers, the Isle of Wight Record Office, the Langham Library, Sunderland Polytechnic, the Kent Archives Office, the Wiltshire Record Office, the Burnley Borough Council, the Trustees of the Godfrey Thomson Unit for Educational Research (Moray House Archives), the Northumberland Record Office, the Norfolk County Council, and the Buckinghamshire Record Office for permission to cite material in their charge.

Finally, I am indebted to Alister Sutherland for patient and thorough criticism of successive drafts.

REFERENCES

[1] pp. 146-7, first edition (London, 1879).

[2] Ibid., p. vii.

[3] For a fuller discussion of this, see Gillian Sutherland and Stephen Sharp, '"The fust official psychologist in the wurrld": aspects of the professionalization of psychology in early twentieth-century Britain', History of Science (forthcoming, June 1980). Cf. also Charles Spearman's presidential address to the Psychology Section of the British Association, reported in Education 4 September 1925, p. 228.

[4] 'Testing for Order and Control in the Corporate Liberal State' reprinted in The I.Q. Controversy ed. Ned Block and Gerald Dworkin, (London, 1977) p.361.

[5] See Gillian Sutherland, 'The magic of measurement: mental testing and English education 1900-1940', Transactions of the Royal Historical Society, 5th ser., xxvii (1977), pp. 135-53.

[6] Olive Banks, Parity and Prestige in English Secondary Education, (London, 1955), p. 129.

[7] These figures supersede the interim figures given in 'The magic of measurement', p. 146. For details of their provenance and the problems of the sources, see Gillian Sutherland, 'Mental testing and education in England and Wales 1880-1940', Applications and Reports to the SSRC, grant HR 4204/2 (January 1976, January 1977, May 1977, May 1978 and December 1978).

[8] It should be stressed that mention of the use of a particular method of selection by a particular authority at any given time does not necessarily mean that that method was employed by the authority for the rest or even a large part of the period 1919-39. Authorities sometimes altered their arrangements with almost bewildering frequency and I find it surprising that the NUT did not attempt to orchestrate a general call for some continuity and stability, for the sake of elementary school teachers and pupils.

[9] It was begun in a paper to the Royal Historical Society in 1976. Stephen Sharp and I continued it subsequently, looking in particular - but mostly in vain - for possible correlations between test use and type of authority, geographical location, density of population etc. We have not been able, so far, to get adequate figures to explore the most interesting possible correlation, that between test use and the number of secondary school places per head of the relevant age group in each Local Education Authority's area. The discussion so far can be followed in detail in 'The magic of measurement' and SSCR HR 4204/2. The full version will be presented in Gillian Sutherland with Stephen Sharp, Ability, Merit and Measurement, to be published at the end of 1981.

[10] Keith Hope, The Political Conception of Merit (to be published by Russell Sage),

ch. 15. I am most grateful to Dr Hope for allowing me to see and refer to this important work.

[11] The Times Educational Supplement October 7, 1913, p. 155.

[12] Education 25 June 1926, p. 677. Cf. also ibid. 8 July 1927, p. 38, Sir D. Milne Watson to the same body.

[13] Ibid., 10 June 1927, p. 679.

[14] The Times Educational Supplement 24 July 1919, p. 375, 'Tests of Intelligence'; ibid. 30 September 1920, p. 521, 'Local Authorities as Innovators'; ibid. 24 December 1921, p. 575, 'National Intelligence Tests'. Cf. also ibid. 26 June 1919, p. 319, review of Stanford-Binet Tests; ibid. 3 July 1919, p. 333, 'Intelligence Tests in Practice'; ibid. 7 April 1921, p. 157, review of Brown and Thomson, The Essentials of Mental Measurement; ibid. 28 January 1922, p. 37, 'New Work in Mental Tests'; ibid. 23 December 1922, p. 557, P. B. Ballard, 'The New Examiner'; Education 20 November 1925, p. 501, comments on use of intelligence tests in British Columbia.

[15] Ibid. 22 July 1927, p. 92. Cf. also The Times Educational Supplement 2 September 1920, p. 480, report of British Association meeting, Section L; Education 24 June 1921, p. 18, report of the AGM of the Association of Headmistresses; ibid. 16 September 1921 pp. 169-70 and The Times Educational Supplement 17 September 1921, p. 415, reports of British Association meetings; ibid. 31 December 1921, p. 582, report of a public debate between Ballard and a member of the British Phrenological Society; ibid. 14 January 1922, p. 21, report of a meeting of the Child Study Society; Education 11 January 1924, p. 23, report of the North of England Education Conference; ibid. 11 September 1925, p. 244, report of British Association meetings; ibid. 10 January 1930, pp. 50 and 52, report of the North of England Education Conference.

[16] Besides the references given above in note 15, see also The Times Educational Supplement 27 August 1921, p. 388, report of lecture programmes in West Riding and in London; ibid. 15 October 1921, p. 458, report of programme of the Notts and District Education Study Society: Education 28 October 1921, p. 242, report of lecture to the Education Guild; The Times Educational Supplement 12 August 1922, p. 376, report of the programme of the Bingley Summer School for Teachers; ibid. 19 August 1922, report of the proceedings of the Brighton Summer School in Psychology; Education 9 September 1927, p. 243, report of British Association meetings.

[17] The Times Educational Supplement 24 April 1919, p. 193, 'The British Psychological Society'.

[18] Education 12 February 1926, p. 180.

[19] Ibid. 3 November 1922, p. 260, 'Dr Hayward and Intelligence Tests'; also The Times Educational Supplement 28 October 1922, p. 474 and 25 November 1922, p. 511. On Hayward in general, see his extraordinary autobiography, F. H. Hayward, An Educational Failure (London, 1938), also A First Book of School Celebrations (both London, 1920). My mother has vivid memories of being inspected by him during her probationary year as a London County Council teacher.

[20] Education 30 January 1920, pp. 82-3 (Adams); The Times Educational Supplement 24 March 1921, p. 132 (Watts); ibid. 19 November 1921, p. 518 (Green); ibid. 7 January 1922, p. 10 (Pear); Education 14 January 1927, pp. 38-40 (Campagnac).

[21] Sutherland, 'The magic of measurement', pp. 141-3, 146-7.

[22] P.H.J.H. Gosden, Education in the Second World War (London, 1976) pp. 238-41.

[23]See Gillian Sutherland, Policy-Making in Elementary Education 1870-95 (London, 1973) esp. pp. 6-9 and chs. 7, 8 and 9.

[24]See A. Tropp, The School Teachers (London, 1957), esp. chs. 7 and 8.

[25]See Sutherland 'The magic of measurement' p. 144; cf. also ibid. p. 151.

[26]Education 15 February 1924, p. 103.

[27]Ibid., 24 April 1925, p. 380.

[28]Ibid., 18 June 1926, pp. 650,52,54,56, AEC debate 'Examinations in Public Schools'; ibid. 25 June 1926, pp. 671-2, 'Authorities - the Schools - and the Children'; ibid. 3 September 1926, pp. 199-200, 'An Individual Examination'; ibid. 22 April 192 , p. 450, NUT Conference, Presidential Address: ibid. 28 January 1927, pp. 116-119, F.F. Potter's speech to the Association of Directors and Secretaries of Education.

[29]Ibid., 2 March 1928, p. 237, 'School Examinations: A More Hopeful Outlook'; ibid. 18 July 1930, pp. 69-69, 'Examinations in Public Elementary Schools'; ibid. 12 December 1930, pp. 555-6, 'Examinations: Their Uses and Abuses'. Even in 1939 the whole thing seemed to be flaring up again over a proposal in Leamington to examine all elementary school leavers - ibid. 10 February 1939, p. 179.

[30]Sutherland, 'The magic of measurement', pp. 149-51.

[31]National Union of Teachers' Library, Hamilton House, Mabledon Place, London W.C.1, Minute Books of the NUT Examinations Board.

[32]Isle of Wight Record Office, Newport, Minutes of the Isle of Wight Examinations Board 1932-39 passim.

[33]Education 4 September 1931, p. 208.

[34]Ibid., 23 November 1923, p. 267; ibid. 22 July 1927, p. 92; ibid. 17 April 1931, p. 460.

[35]Langham Library, Sunderland Polytechnic, Sunderland, Minutes of Sunderland County Borough Council Higher Education Sub-Committee 17 May 1922; see also ibid. 13 October 1921.

[36]Ibid. 17 May 1922 and 18 October 1927; Public Record Office, Ed. 77/40.

[37]Public Record Office, Ed 77/126,/127,/128 and 110/84. Cf. also Education 5 September 1930, p. 200, 'Substitute for Examinations'.

[38]For example, County Hall, Martineau Lane, Norwich, Minutes Norfolk County Council Education Committee, 14 January 1922, minute 13, esp. (c); Buckinghamshire Record Office, Aylesbury, Minutes Buckinghamshire County Council Scholarship and General Purposes Sub-Committee 20 June 1929 and 15 December 1932: Public Record Office, Ed 77/21 (Isle of Ely, 1924), Ed 110/5 (Cheshire, 1933), Ed 77/45 (Gloucestershire, 1928), Ed 77/51 (Herefordshire, 1927 - where HMIs recommend that the oral conducted by the secondary school head teachers should include questions of this type), Ed 77/60 (Bury, 1928), Ed 77/87 and Ed 77/88 (Bath, 1924 and 1932), Ed 77/117 (Worcester, 1929) and Ed 77/124 (Dewsbury, 1927). Some of the external examiners employed also conducted their oral examinations in similar fashion - see, for example, Public Record Office. Ed 77/23 (Cheshire, 1923), Ed 77/26 (Stockport, 1928), Ed 77/118 (E. Riding of Yorkshire, 1925) and Ed 77/119 (Hull, 1924).

[39]The Times Educational Supplement 28 May 1921, p. 240.

[40]Ibid. 4 June 1921, p. 252, 11 June 1921, p. 264 and 18 June 1921, p. 280.

[41]Education 6 February 1920, pp. 102-3.

[42]E.g. The Times Educational Supplement 12 February 1920, p. 92, 'Secondary School Notes'; Education 10 April 1925, pp. 346-7, R. B. Henderson, 'Some aspects of the Scholarship System'; ibid. 23 December 1927, p. 609, 'Secondary School Notes'; ibid. 28 April 1933, p. 486, 'Notes from the Association of Assistant Mistresses'; ibid. 29 June 1934, pp. 747-8, 'School Examinations'; ibid. 19 November 1937, pp. 534-7, 'Report of the Joint Advisory Committee of the Association of Education Committees and the Four Secondary Associations', esp. p. 535, terms of reference (c). For examples of the extensive involvement of secondary school head teachers and staff in the selection process see Public Record Office, Ed 77/28 (Cornwall, 1925), Ed 77/29 (Cumberland, 1928), Ed 77/30 (Carlisle, 1924), Ed 77/33 (Devon, 1925), Ed 77/34 (Exeter, 1924), Ed 77/38 (Gateshead, 1929), Ed 77/40 (Sunderland, 1927), Ed 77/41 (West Hartlepool, 1927), Ed 77/48 (Portsmouth, 1924), Ed 77/49 (Southampton, 1932), Ed 77/50 (Isle of Wight, 1927), Ed 77/54 (Lancashire, 1927), Ed 77/58 (Bolton, 1929), Ed 77/61 (Liverpool, 1923), Ed 77/65 (Preston, 1926), Ed 77/66 (Rochdale, 1928), Ed 77/68 (Southport, 1928), Ed 77/74 (Lincolnshire, Kesteven, 1923), Ed 77/75 (Lincolnshire, Kesteven, 1934), Ed 77/91 (Tynemouth, 1924), Ed 77/99 (Staffordshire, 1929), Ed 77/100 (Stoke on Trent, 1928), Ed 77/102 (Wolverhampton, 1923), Ed 77/137 (Isle of Man, 1935) and Ed 110/110 (Smethwick, 1934).

[43]Cf. Education 13 December 1935, pp. 580-2, Annie Lloyd-Evans, 'Psychology in the Training of Teachers' (paper presented to the British Association).

[44]Ibid., 30 July 1926, p. 11.

[45]Ibid., 20 March 1936, pp. 348-50; ibid. 12 February 1937, pp. 190, 194-5; ibid. 9 July 1937, pp. 35-6; ibid. 10 September 1937, p. 252; ibid. 3 December 1937, p. 584; ibid. 4 November 1938, p. 479.

[46]Ibid., 4 November 1938, p. 479.

[47]Sutherland, Policy-Making, ch. 3.

[48]Education 21 November 1924, pp. 369-70 (Hey); ibid. 13 February 1925, pp. 158-9 (Sharp); ibid. 30 July 1926, p. 116 (Pickles); ibid. 30 January 1931. pp. 132-3 (Boyce); ibid. 8 January 1932, pp. 32-3 (Walling).

[49]Ibid., 17 July 1925, pp. 74-5 (Gater); Malcolm Seaborne, 'William Brockington, Director of Education for Leicestershire 1903-47' in Brian Simon ed., Education in Leicesterhsire 1540-1940 (Leicester, 1968), pp. 195-226; Toby Weaver, 'Education: Retrospect and Prospect', Cambridge Journal of Education ix (1979), pp. 3-4, 6-7 and Harry Ree, Educator Extraordinary: The Life and Achievements of Henry Morris 1889-1961 (London, 1973) esp. pp. 7-11 (Innes, Davies and Morris).

[50]For Leicestershire, see Seaborne, op. cit.; for Kent, see Public Record Office, Ed 77/53 and Kent Archives Office, County Hall, Maidstone, C/E 10/14, C/E 10/15, The Kent Education Gazette February 1934 pp. 157-60, March 1934 pp. 182-3, January 1935 pp. 133-6. For Wiltshire, see Wiltshire Record Office, County Hall, Trowbridge, Minutes General Education Committee 25 November 1932, minute 809 and 28 July 1933, minutes 365 and 366; Minutes Pupil Records Sub-Committee, notes of meeting 28 April 1934 and interim Report 16 June 1934; I. M. Slocombe, Wiltshire Education Department to the author 12 May 1975 - in response to a nationally distributed questionnaire about test use (CSQ 1975).

[51]Education 16 January 1931, pp. 62, 64.

[52]Town Hall, Burnley, Minutes Burnley County Borough Council Higher Education Sub-Committee March 1922 and Minutes Burnley CBC Schools Sub-Committee

25 February 1925. Cf. also the Burnley entry in Sir Philip Hartog and Gladys Roberts, A Conspectus of Examinations in Great Britain and Northern Ireland (London. International Institute Examinations Enquiry, 1937) s.1A.

[53] For Bradford, see Public Record Office, Ed 77/123. For Newcastle, see Edinburgh University Library, Moray House Archives, Index to users of Moray House group intelligence tests (M.H.Ts.) and Newcastle-upon-Tyne Education Department reply to CSQ 1975.

[54] For a fuller discussion of London, see Sutherland, 'The magic of measurement' pp. 150-1 and Sutherland and Sharp '"The fust official psychologist in the wurrld"'.

[55] Bryan Keith-Lucas, English Local Government in the Nineteenth and Twentieth Centuries (London. The Historical Association, 1977) p. 23. For detailed studies of particular localities see J. M. Lee, Social Leaders and Public Persons. A study of county government in Cheshire since 1888 (Oxford, 1963) and G. W. Jones, Borough Politics: A Study of the Wolverhampton Town Council 1884-1964 (London, 1969).

[56] P.H.J.H. Gosden and P. R. Sharp, The Development of an Education Service: The West Riding 1889-1974 (Oxford, 1979) pp. 23-4 (Jackson); Education 24 April 1925, pp. 388-9 (Raley); ibid. 23 January 1925, pp. 92-3 (Kenrick).

[57] Ibid.. 17 June 1932, p. 697. For the working coalition formed between Rowlinson, Sir Percy Jackson, Brockington, Lady Simon and R. H. Tawney on the Consultative Committee ofthe Board of Education in the 1930s, see Joan Simon, 'The Shaping of the Spens Report on Secondary Education 1933-38: An Inside View', British Journal of Education Studies xxv (1977) pp. 63-80, 170-85.

[58] Education 9 June 1939, pp. 706-7.

[59] Ibid., 24 June 1938, p. 825; ibid. 23 June 1939, pp. 807, 809, 811. Cf. also ibid. 10 January 1936, p. 27.

[60] See above, p. 81.

[61] The Times Educational Supplement 3 February 1921, p. 54: Northumberland Record Office, Melton Park, North Gosforth, Newcastle-upon-Tyne, Minutes of the Scholarships and Exhibitions Sub-Committee 27 January 1921, minute 2; Notes from 1956 and 1957 for lectures on selection procedures by Mr G. Bosomworth, formerly Examinations Officer for Northumberland Education Committee and kindly made available to the author by Mr Bosomworth and the Director of Education for Northumberland in response to CSQ 1975.

[62] Public Record Office, Ed 77/123.

[63] Karier, 'Testing for Order and Control', p. 346.

[64] Report of the Schools Inquiry Commission P.P. 1867-8 xxvii, p. 95. For a more extended discussion see Gillian Sutherland, 'Secondary Education: The Education of the Middle Classes' in Gillian Sutherland ed., Government and Society in Nineteenth-Century Britain: Commentaries on British Parliamentary Papers: Education (Dublin, 1977) pp. 137-66. Cf. also Hope, The Political Conception of Merit.

[65] The Times Educational Supplement 16 September 1910, p. 19, 'The New Secondary Education'.

[66] Education 2 January 1925, p. 7.

[67] Is this, incidentally, very different from the objectives some of us have - and occasionally articulate - when interviewing prospective university entrants?

[68] Education 18 March 1938, pp. 332-4 'Special Places in Secondary Schools', p. 332. By this time 36 LEAs were offering 100% special places.

[69] Ibid., 19 June 1936, pp. 807, 808, 810, 812, 814, 816, 818; Councillor Hyman's comment is quoted on p. 812; cf. also the remarks of Councillor Tuck of Lincoln on p. 814 and the dispute at Brighton described in the reference in n. 68 above.

[70] The Times Educational Supplement 5 October 1915, p. 119, 'A Necessary Revolution', 2 November 1915, p. 131, 'The Ways and Means of Revolution', 13 December 1917, p. 481, 'Some National Aspects of Childhood', 14 November 1918, p. 489, 'Education during the War', 28 October 1920, p. 575, 'Two Steps in Secondary Education'.

[71] Quoted in Education 12 May 1922, p. 282.

[72] Ibid., 8 January 1926, p. 24, J. F. Duff to the Eugenics Education Society; ibid. October 1928, p. 290, R. B. Henderson, 'Some Reflections on the Scholarship System'; ibid. 14 September 1934,p. 228, Dr Cyril Norwood to the British Association; cf. also ibid. 3 December 1937, p. 585, 'Local Authority Notes'.

[73] Ibid. 21 October 1932, pp. 378-80, 'Selection for and Tuition Fees in Secondary Schools'. Cf. also ibid. 13 January 1933 p. 41 (from the comments of Percival Sharp, now Secretary of the AEC to the North of England Conference), ibid. 23 June 1933, p. 708 (from the presidential address of Alderman Rowlinson to the AEC AGM) and ibid. 18 March 1938, p. 332 (the arguments at Brighton).

[74] Ibid. 19 June 1936, p. 807.

THERAPEUTIC USES OF ILLUSIONS
A CRITIQUE OF THE PSYCHO-SOCIAL IDEOLOGY OF OTTO RANK

Clarence J. Karier
Professor, Department of Educational Policy Studies
College of Education, University of Illinois
Champaign-Urbana

ABSTRACT

This paper is part of a larger work which deals with the change in western culture from a predominant Christian oriented culture to that of a predominant secular culture. Within this shift there occurred both a transformation of the dominant moral ideology as well as a significant change in the professional class which interprets that ideology in everyday life. While in the past Christian era it was the theologian who played this role, now in the secular city of the twentieth century it was more often the psychologist who came to play that role. Just as in the past when different kinds of religions held competing ideological assumptions which resulted in different social consequences so in the therapeutic society different kinds of psychologies hold different kinds of assumptions resulting in a variety of social consequences. Thus in the therapeutic society where sickness replaces sinfulness, the role of psychologists as interpreters of human experience can be critically analyzed with respect to their assumptions about human nature and society as well as their construction of social reality. This paper deals with only one small segment of the psychoanalytic movement reflected in the work of Otto Rank. Otto Rank was a student and close associate of Sigmund Freud for many years. Eventually he came to America and had a significant impact on the practice of psychological therapy as well as social work in America. What follows is a critique of certain characteristics of his psycho-social ideas.

****

Shortly before Otto Rank died in 1939, Erich Fromm published an article in which he argued that '... the basic trend of Rank's philosophy is akin to Fascist philosophy'.[1] He believed this to be the case even though Rank himself was not politically a fascist; nor did he appear to have any '... intention of copying the Nazi formula'. Fromm further puzzled over the problem of why so many American social workers had found Rank's ideas so attractive. He closed his analysis by suggesting two intriguing hypotheses. First he suggested '... that this acceptance of Rank seems to indicate the inroads that Fascist philosophy can make, if only it avoids mention of those political symbols which made it unacceptable to liberals and Jews'.[2] Secondly, he surmised that Rank's thought might appear attractive to psychiatric social workers because in the frustration of their day-to-day work in which they attempt to help their clients overcome their emotional problems they are often confronted with economic realities which are insolvable at times. Given such social circumstances, Rank's 'will therapy' which suggests that the patient must learn to live with his or her illusions might appear as a welcome panacea.

In the fifty years since Fromm published his critique, America has engaged in a hot war against fascism and a cold war against communism, out of which has emerged a highly militarized multinational corporate superstructure. Within this economic structure America has developed a complementary therapeutic social welfare-oriented society with all its thousands of 'helping' psycho-social services. Given this context, it might be profitable to once again consider not only some of the issues which Fromm's analysis raised, but to critically examine the philosophic underpinnings of Rank's psychology and its possible social implications. In this paper I will therefore first analyze what Fromm believed to be the 'fascist philosophy' which he saw in Rank's thought; consider these ideas in a broader nineteenth and twentieth century cultural context; discuss the problem of definition; analyze the psycho-social ideas of Rank as he historically developed them; and lastly suggest possible ways Rankian thought and therapy might be interpreted as reflecting deeper historic currents of the modern therapeutically oriented welfare society.

I

In analyzing Rank's thought, Fromm made no attempt at a comprehensive description of fascist philosophy, but confined his argument to what he considered some 'essential features' and demonstrated that these ideas appeared in Rank's philosophy. The fascist, Fromm argued, lived in a nihilistic world where the search for truth is not only vain but harmful for most people. Reality itself is thought to be illusory. In such a basically non-rational world, leadership emerges which creatively welds the illusions of the masses for action and thus the power and strength of arms replaces the power of truth, while the realities of injustice and suffering are taken as a given, not susceptible to rational reform. The fascist prides himself or herself on being a 'realist', fundamentally accepting the world of power relationships as given and readily adapts to its demands. Idealism rests with creative leaders who bring along the herd. Within this view emerges a thoroughly authoritarian outlook which sees the social world in terms of powerful and powerless, superior and inferior, strong and weak. Leadership thus rests not on truth, education or rational social values but rather on proven ability to creatively use the illusions of the masses to exercise power. These, then, were some of the 'essential features' which Fromm thought he saw in Rank's 'dynamic psychology'.

Was Rank, then, a closet fascist or was he possibly a fascist without knowing it? He personally did not approve of the label as Fromm was using it with respect to himself. From a former patient, Rank had heard that in a lecture Fromm identified him as holding a fascist philosophy.[3] In a letter to Jessie Taft, Rank remarked in no uncertain terms 'I don't like it'.[4]

In what sense, then, might one agree or disagree with Fromm? Much, of course, depends on definition. Fromm was not claiming that Rank was politically a fascist nor was he claiming that Rank himself would agree with his analysis. He was insisting, however, that there was such a thing as a fascist philosophy and that Rank held many of its basic tenets. In the context of the times, when many thought they knew what fascism was, this might have seemed straight forward enough. However, in our present day such a charge might appear highly questionable. This is due, in part at least, to our usage of the term over the last four decades which has served to so objuscate its meaning as to make many people wary of its use altogether.

In the intervening years the term fascism has become for many a synonym for all that is evil, eliciting painful memories of such infamous centers of human degradation as Auschwitz, Buchenwald, Dachau and Belsen. So taken, the term is reserved to describe a specific instant in history. For some, any use of the term beyond that specific usage significantly detracts from the memorialization of the victims which is their due. Others prefer simply to bury the term with the historic dead. Thus assuming that history does not repeat itself, fascism can safely be viewed as having come to an end with the defeat of the Axis powers in 1945.

In the opposite direction, there are those who render the term useless by making it applicable to virtually any and all of one's enemies.[5] Still others define fascism in terms dialectically related to their own ideological position. Nolte,[6] for example, in The Three Faces of Fascism (1966) points out how our ideology influences our definition of fascism. He argues:

> Christian theorists see fascism as part of the secularization of society as man turns from God; but this implies that the antidote to fascism is theocracy. Conservatives regard fascism as the revolt of the masses against current values, yearning with pessimistic nostalgia for the 'good old days'. Liberals regard fascism as a form of totalitarianism, and are, as a result, incapable of distinguishing between fascism and Stalinism. Nationalists look upon fascism as either a high or a low point in national history, and are therefore prey to conservative or ultra-right nostalgia for an earlier epoch. Marxists view fascism as the product of the contradictions in advanced capitalism, and hence see the abolition of bourgeois society as the necessary precondition for the elimination of fascist tendencies.[7]

In lieu of all these ideological interpretations, Nolte offers his own 'nonpartisan theory' which '... sees fascism as a specific and supra-national phenomenon of a particular epoch'.[8] He does this, he asserts, so as to make possible 'discarding the burden of the past'. Nolte's 'nonpartisan theory' does essentially that. It effectively buries the term in a particular epoch under The Three Faces of Fascism and thus frees the present from the 'burden of the past'.[9]

The issue of definition is complicated not only by the ideology of the interpreter but also by the particular discipline of the interpreter. Thus it seems clear that Nicos Poulantzas' exceptional political-economic treatment in Fascism and Dictatorism fails to treat the intellectual and cultural dimensions of fascism just as George Mosse's excellent treatment of the intellectual and cultural roots of this subject in The Crisis of German Ideology fails to relate the intellectual roots to the emerging corporate structure which we now know played such an important practical role in the rise and early success of national socialism.[10] Monopoly capitalism in the form of multinational corporations and cartel arrangements provided the economic superstructure within which fascism was nourished and the spread of communism checked. For example, in 1939 Adolph Hitler quite appropriately awarded General Motors' chief executive for overseas operation the Order of the German Eagle (first class). It was after all G.M. through their Open truck facility at the Brandenburg complex who significantly helped put the 'blitz' into the Wehrmacht with their 'Blitz' trucks.[11] Together G.M. and Ford subsidiaries 'built nearly 90 per cent of the armored "mule" 3-ton half-tracks and more than 70 per cent of the Reich's medium and heavy-duty trucks'.[12] At their Russelsheim facility, G.M. produced the first operational jet engine for the Luftwaffe.[13] After the war this same G.M. demanded and received from the U.S. Government 33 million dollars in reparations for damage done to their plants by Allied bombing during the war.[14] G.M.'s multinational role in the development of German air and ground transport before, during and after the war is, itself, no less impressive than the role Exxon played in building Ethyl tetraethyl plants in Germany[15] and the assistance that Standard Oil gave to I. G. Farben, the builder and developer of Auschwitz, in creating the facilities for the production of synthetic nitrates, fuels and rubber.[16]

Monopoly capitalism, with its international cartel arrangements and multinational corporations, was and still is a vital part of the economic framework within which the fascist state has emerged in the twentieth century. Any comprehensive treatment of fascism in this century must treat the developing economic structure of the West with all its tensions and relate those tensions to the political, intellectual and cultural trends of that era.[17] Leon Trotsky was correct it seems in The Struggle Against Fascism in Germany when he argued that even though the economic structure and fascism were intimately related, it is just as much a mistake to view fascism as inevitably flowing from monopoly capitalism in some predetermined sense as it is equally a mistake to see fascism in virtually all political and social movements. Nevertheless, it also seems as much an error to divorce monopoly capitalism from fascism as it is to refrain from using the term altogether. The relationships might better be recognized as complex, subtle and at times transactional, limited by considerable historical contingencies.

As historians and social scientists develop a more adequate picture of fascism, it seems the term is best treated as a composite picture of a many-sided condition of man in the stream of twentieth century history. Within that stream there exists a meta-culture, dynamically born anew with the passing of each generation which helps define and structure the conscious realities of the emerging world. Given this overarching structure, we can then isolate people, movements and institutions for analysis purposes and thus see some people who perhaps were more sensitive to some of the ideological currents that ultimately could logically and in many ways historically did seem to support the political and economic development of fascism, without themselves being fascist. By the same token, we may analyze the ideology of a given person without making causal claims for either the ideology or the structure in which it exists, but merely assume some kind of unexplored transactional relationship to exist between culture, economic structure and political action. In this respect many of the ideas of such notable people as G. Stanley Hall, D. H. Lawrence and indeed, Otto Rank as Erich Fromm saw him, can be viewed as expressions of some of the main cultural currents which have tended to shape our developing fascist world.

II

While in a very real sense fascism was a response to the condition of life in the twentieth century, it was also a culmination of a larger nineteenth century revolution against Enlightenment values. That European liberal bourgeoisie which so confidently stood on the barricades of social change at the beginning of the nineteenth century now at the end of the century stood in frozen narcistic contemplation of its own destruction. What began as a romantic reaction to the rationalism of the Enlightenment at the beginning of the nineteenth century culminated at the end of that century in a storm of intellectual nihilism. Western society, in its search for certainty in an uncertain world, had in its weary disillusionment rediscovered irrationalism in more profound and despairing ways than anything the West had experienced since the decline of the ancient world. Literate intelligence would henceforth focus not on the jobs of life and the future millennium, but, rather on the crisis of death and the absurd existence of man alienated from 'culture', 'nature', or 'God'.

By the time Nietzsche had passed beyond tragedy, beyond good and evil, Kierkegaard had discovered the value of Fear and Trembling, and Melville had emphasized the indestructible nature of evil, Dostoevsky had written, 'There are three powers, three powers alone, able to conquer and to hold captive forever the conscience of these impotent rebels for their happiness - those forces are miracle, mystery, and authority'.[18] A transformation of values had occurred which would focus on the absurdidy of life and the irrational wellspring of human motivations and actions. The alienated unfulfilled world of the bourgeoisie held little promise for the coming generation.

Individual existence was to be secured, not by fulfilling one's duties to the mass or herd, which lived by illusions nor by placing one's faith in the humanitarian future nor in the rationalistic past, but, rather, by the sheer assertion of one's self in a nihilistic world. In the name of sincerity and authenticity, all ideology had to be rejected. Youth without banner, youth without cause became the rallying cry of the new generation. In such a view, representative democracy came to mean nothing more than a bourgeois facade behind which petty, selfish, vested interests developed. Democracy appeared to be a sham when one passed beyond appearances to the reality of nihilism. Even science, the goddess of the Enlightenment, which once offered so much rational hope for a suffering humanity, came to be viewed as a Frankenstein monster, ushering in an age of mass organization and mass culture that threatened to destroy individual identity.

Within this zeitgeist, Otto Rank as a youth of nineteen mused, '... if anything could drive me to suicide, it would be the stupidity and commonness of mankind'.[19] Born into a lower middle class, culturally barren, unhappy home, with a father who drank too much and a family that fought too much,[20] Otto Rank developed an image of himself that provided the personality structure upon which he hung the ideological values which sustained him throughout his lifetime. In many ways his was to be a life of escape. So distasteful was his family experience that he could not bear to carry his father's name, changing it as quickly as he could from Rosenfeld to Rank. As a youth, Rank escaped the unfortunate family situation by delving into poetry, music and philosophy and by nurturing an inflated conception of himself as a creative artistic genuis who would one day stand against the commonness of mankind. He said, 'I feel for most people no sympathy, only for animals'.[21] He felt he was called to commune with the truly great. 'Just as whole races of average men prepare unconsciously for the possibility of the coming of the one superior being, so must I slowly and unconscious of the goal go through a lot of average works in order to reach the worthwhile ones'.[22]

Rank eventually found those 'worthwhile ones' when he encountered the works of Arthur Schopenhauer, Richard Wagner and Friedrich Nietzsche. Schopenhauer helped him discover the negative side of the 'will' buried deep in the recesses of the unconscious mind. With Nietzsche he found the Dionysus 'will' which could carry him beyond the good and evil of the herd. In Wagner he communed with the creative artist who could so admirably unite 'tone and word' with 'dramatic action'. All confirmed in their own way his youthful contempt for humanity as well as his search for a super soul, or what late in life he called a 'God-man'. Throughout his life these three men provided the basic foundation upon which he constructed his philosophy as well as his psychology. This philosophy was, in turn, congruent with his personal psychological temperament which consistently propelled him into extreme states of elation as well as depression. Nietzsche served him well when he was at the mountain top enjoying his grandiose view, while Schopenhauer guided his path in the darker valleys of depression.

In all of this he saw himself as an artist, indeed, much of which Rank wrote about the artist can be easily translated as autobiographical. From his early conception of the artist in his youthful diary, to his Der Kunstler which he used to introduce himself to Freud, to his more mature work, Art and Artist, the basic structure of the artistic act of creation remained the same. On April 29, 1905, he wrote in his youthful diary:

> One can't bring up an artist ... The artist in the act of their creation fluctuates for the most part between life and death; he 'chooses' between suicide and creating, between art and hysteria; if there is a grain too much of resistance, if the delivery does not occur at the right time, then the artist falls. But even if all that were possible, who would unburden on his son so many severe hardships, suffering that goes psychically as well as physically to the uttermost limits of life, which are, however, necessary to many a great artist.[23]

Rank considered himself a 'great artist' who had personally chosen between 'suicide and creating, between art and hysteria'. Jessie Taft accurately notes that at this point in time a complete organization of his views was taking place. On May 10, 1905, he wrote, 'It comes only to this, that one has the courage to universalize his experience; whoever has this courage, his generalizations are correct'.[24] Finally, on May 13, 1905, Der Kunstler was born: 'Now I see everything clearly: the world process is no longer a riddle; I can explain the whole culture, yes, I can explain everything. What shall I be able to do with the remainder of my life?'.[25] Der Kunstler became Rank's statement of his ideological beliefs to which he would return again and again during his professional career.

When Alfred Adler, Rank's family physician, introduced him to Freud it was his essay on 'The Artist' which he gave to Freud as a means of introduction. Freud recalled,

> One day a young man who had passed through the technical training school introduced himself with a manuscript which showed very unusual comprehension. We induced him to go through the Gymnasium and the University and to devote himself to the nonmedical side of psychoanalytic investigation The little society acquired in him a zealous and dependable secretary and I gain in Otto Rank a faithful helper and co-worker.[26]

For the next twenty years Rank served Freud as a '.... research worker, his proof reader, and his adopted son'.[27] Throughout these years Freud educated Rank by sending him to the University of Vienna where he completed his Ph D thesis on Richard Wagner entitled Die Lohengrin Sage. He moved quickly into Freud's secret inner circle which, after Jung's and Adler's disaffection, had become so important in directing the psychoanalytic movement.[28] Concerned with practical application of psychoanalysis, Hanns Sachs and Rank founded The Imago and shortly thereafter Rank became editor of Zeitschrift. As a bright, intuitively inclined young man, Rank grew very close to Freud, acting at times as virtually his corresponding secretary and personal aide. So highly regarded was Rank that Freud put him in charge of four revised editions of The Interpretations of Dreams. Thus educated in the field of psychoanalysis by Freud himself, perceived as creative, hardworking and trustworthy in every respect it seemed clear to many that Rank was being groomed to succeed Freud as the leader of the psychoanalytic movement. Throughout these very productive years, 1905-1925, both men profited from each other's thoughts. Freud came to especially appreciate Rank's intuitive insights. As Rank did imaginative work on The Double in literature and published The Myth of the Birth of the Hero, in which Freud contributed an essay, it also seemed apparent that Freud saw this work as an extension of much of his own work. This is exactly what Freud wanted: someone to imaginatively develop the powerful and fruitful concepts which lay imbedded in the psychoanalytic paradigm. Perhaps it was this wish which led him to seriously misjudge the direction his young student had taken from the very start. Rank was not content with simply exploring the nonmedical side of the psychoanalytic paradigm, but rather was developing his own paradigm - a paradigm based not on the rationalized world of Freud, but on the irrational world of Schopenhauer, Wagner and Nietzsche. The difference was fundamental.

The inevitable break began when Rank presented a completed manuscript to Freud called The Trauma of Birth in honor of his birthday on May 6, 1923. The break was completed when Rank sent Freud a decoratively bound copy of Nietzsche's work for his seventieth birthday in 1926. The meaning of this latter gift was made clear when, three years later in Truth and Reality, Rank said, 'Nietzsche, who experienced thoroughly the whole tragedy of the creative man and admitted in his "amor fati" the willingness to pay for it, is in my opinion the first and has been up to now the only psychologist'.[29]

In The Trauma of Birth, Rank was following Freud's earlier suggestion that the source of anxiety might possibly originate in the act of birth. However, he went considerably farther when he put the critical emphasis on the mother and the infant child's relationship to the mother. Karl Abraham, Ernest Jones and others within the inner circle were quick to sense a serious heresy in the making. Freud, however, was reluctant to make a clearcut judgment. While he hesitated, he entertained Rank's thesis, argued, discussed and attempted to persuade. Almost to the very end of the final break Freud held out hope that Rank could be expected to return.[30] Once again Freud was wrong. Rank set out on his own, establishing his practice in Paris and then taking an extended trip to America where he lectured, gave seminars and presented what, in effect, were his own ideas about psychoanalysis and therapy. What followed was an agonizing period in which Rank swung from a position of rebellious son to one of total submissiveness, publicly recanting his deviation, to once again rejecting Freud's position outright. In the midst of severe depression, Rank returned to Vienna where in many hours of consultation with Freud, both he and Freud became convinced that his rebellion was brought about because of his 'manic state' which was triggered by the announcement of Freud's dangerous illness.[31] Rank sent a letter of apology to the inner circle, while Freud wrote optimistically that he believed much of the problem had been resolved. Of course it was not. As Freud suggested that Rank undergo analysis and Rank refused, the letters between the two became biting and bitter.

Increasingly as Freud engaged Rank, he vacillated in his interpretation of what was actually taking place. He initially refused to recognize what was clearly a highly significant deviation. Later he attempted to explain the situation in terms of Rank's neurotic reaction to the announcement of his cancer,[32] while still later he accounted for much of the problem in terms of Rank's need for money, thus establishing himself in an independent practice in Paris and New York City. Lastly, in Moses and Monotheism, he analyzed the Rank case as,

> A young man whose fate it was to grow up besides a worthless father (who) began by developing, in defiance of him, into a capable, trustworthy and honorable person. In the prime of life his character was reversed, and thenceforward he behaved as though he had taken this same father as a model. In ... the beginning of such a course of events there is always an identification with the father in early childhood. This is afterwards repudiated, and even overcompensated, but in the end establishes itself once more.[33]

Was Rank's conflict with Freud precipitated by the excessive spending habits of Rank's wife, Tola, as Freud once suggested;[34] was it caused by Rank's neurotic reaction to the announcement of Freud's cancer which for a time both Rank and Freud seemed to believe;[35] was it another patterned, stoicly tragic case of fathers (real or adopted) and sons as Freud later suggested in Moses and Monotheism; was it a case of a creative young scholar growing beyond his teacher and the teacher not being able to adjust graciously to the situation as Jessie Taft suggested:[36] or was she even more correct when she later suggested that an adoption of a particular psychology is more like an adoption of religion than a science?[37] While many of these reasons are not mutually exclusive and may be viewed as interactive factors in the events which transpired, it seems clear that the announcement of Freud's cancer and Rank's deviation was an unfortunate coincidence which allowed some interpreters to put negative connotations on Rank's motivations. For example, the announcement of Freud's cancer could hardly have influenced Rank's writing of The Trauma of Birth which was finished in April of 1923, the same month which Rank was first informed of Freud's illness. Rank's deviation, at least in The Trauma of Birth, clearly was not caused by the impact of the announcement of Freud's cancer. It is more reasonable to recognize that the ideas developed by Rank in The Trauma of Birth were developed, in fact, over a long period of time, even though they had not been fully discussed within the inner circle. Moreover, in spite of the highly charged reactions of the historic actors and the strong personal ties which at times clouded the issues, it seems more reasonable to recognize that from the outset Rank was moving from a basically different ideological position and as a consequence was clearly developing a profoundly different psychology. This psychology ultimately had to be rejected by Freud regardless of his personal attachment to Rank. It was not just a matter of growth and development either, because much of that which was implicit in his earlier thought was simply later made explicit.

Psychoanalysis provided Rank with a vehicle to imaginatively play with religious symbols, literature, philosophy and anthropological data, but it was not the hard core structure out of which his view of the universe was built. While psychoanalysis could be used to embellish that universe the hard core structure was still derived not from Freud, but from Schopenhauer, Wagner and Nietzsche. Where Freud emphasized the importance of reason, Rank emphasized the importance of will, and where Freud saw the search for truth and its ultimate acceptance as constructively therapeutic, Rank saw the search for truth as ultimately destructive and the creation and acceptance of illusions as therapeutic. These were no minor misunderstandings. Not only did Rank come to emphasize the role of the mother over that of the father in the life of the child long before it was made more fashionable by others such as Eric Erickson to do so, but he gradually came to argue, as did Sandor Ferenczi and others, that therapy was more important than theory, and that understanding the immediate present of the patient is far more important for therapeutic purposes than understanding the patient's past history.

On virtually every significant construct, Rank had reversed positions with Freud. While on some of the weaker concepts of psychoanalysis, such as Freud's treatment of the artist, Rank constructed his psychology of the neurotic as a misbegotten artist. Rank, however, was not simply a youthful rebel bent on upstaging his former master at any price. His view of reality, philosophy and psychology were fundamentally different. The cleavage between Freud and Rank went far deeper than merely a difference between two psychologists, rather it represented a fundamental rift in western thinking which has persisted to the present day.

III

The idea that reason could light the path to truth within the human soul as well as the social order and that such a path was the desired path to virtue was itself the ideological keystone in the triumphant enlightenment arch of progress, under which so many western thinkers had passed. It was this keystone which gave way under the pressure of the contradictions inherent in alienated bourgeois life by the end of the century. While Rank's thought was an expression of a new 'modern' 20th century consciousness it also reflected a fundamental break with the enlightenment belief in progress. That belief was firmly based on the ancient Socratic rationalistic dictum that the unexamined life was not worth living, which not only assumed that truth was possible but that the pursuit of truth was a valued 'good' because in the end both the individual and the community would be better for it.

No Greek could conceive of the separation of the individual self from the community in which that self was nourished as so many today are inclined to do. The examination of life for Socrates and many western thinkers was not only that of an analysis of the individual, but equally as important, an analysis of the community in which he or she developed. Both Freud and Marx clearly worked within this tradition. Together they continued to assume that the search for truth was not only possible but desirable. However, both also lived and thought within the broader zeitgeist of a nineteenth century economic world that in revolutionizing production and consumption had profoundly shaken the roots of the western mind at the same time. The crisis of the bourgeoisie, translated in terms of European romanticism or American transcendentalism so conceptually split the individual from the social world that western man could now begin to perceive the individual as something separate and apart from the social order and the social order as something separate from the individual. In this context Freud's analysis of the individual and Marx's analysis of the social order were possible. In a sense Marx to a limited extent and Freud to a greater extent were now doing something no Greek could do. Both worked within a world view which, beginning with Rousseau, could mentally separate the individual from society. To be sure, neither Freud nor Marx could conceive of the individual as humanly possible without society. The entire corpus of their works stand as benchmarks of the extent to which the zeitgeist of the romantic's split view of life had managed to penetrate western rationalistic consciousness. Marx saw the problem of alienation and constantly insisted on conceptually putting men back into history. His search was for understanding the dynamics of men's social relations which he came to believe caused alienation. While Marx in the early part of the century sought to discover the social condition which gave rise to the phenomenon of alienation reflected in early romantic literature as well as Hegelian philosophy, Freud created psychoanalysis in the context of the neoromantic zeitgeist at the end of the century. By Freud's time the separation of the individual from society was even more acceptable to western consciousness.[38]

Psychoanalysis can and often is viewed as akin to the romantic frame of mind because of its approach to mental phenomena with its reliance on the unconscious for a more genuine source of truth. The emphasis on free association can also be viewed as a variant of the romantic inner voice. While the very idea of individual happiness necessarily standing in an antagonistic relationship to the social order as the basis from which mental energy is converted in sublimated form was, itself, not fully realizable, without a romantic sense of alienated reality to begin with.[39] Under the circumstances, even the creative activity of the artist is viewed as rooted in estrangement and therefore a variant of neurotic behaviour. All these characteristics of psychoanalysis clearly suggest romantic underpinnings. However, Freud and his psychoanalytic view of the human condition was also firmly rooted in biological science which carried with it an enlightenment faith in science and the promise of the intelligibility of truth. This truth could not only be empirically and rationally discovered in terms of public knowledge, but it was further assumed that it was, in fact, desirable to do so. This, then, was the common ground upon which the two great rationalists of the nineteenth century worked. While Marx sought to understand the social dynamic which governed the creation of our social system and Freud sought to understand the patterns and structures which govern the individual psyche, both assumed that a truth existed behind the facade of appearances that was intelligible and worth knowing.[40] As sons of the Enlightenment they believed that illusions were the chains which had kept men in bondage. Where Marx saw the damaging effects of 'false consciousness', Freud saw the crippling consequences of 'rationalizations'. Both believed in the therapeutic value of truth.

When Marx wrote of religion as the 'opium of the people' he argued that, 'The abolition of religion, as the illusory happiness of men, is a demand for their real happiness. The call to abandon their illusions about their condition is a call to abandon a condition which requires illusions'.[41] So too, after a lengthy discussion of religion as a form of illusion, Freud ended his work by insisting, 'No, our science is no illusion. But an illusion it would be to suppose that what science cannot give us we can get elsewhere'.[42]

Standing in the midst of the crumbling ideological ruins of the Christian state at the dawning of the secular state, both men knew the power of illusions and the varied ways false consciousness could be manipulated for the happiness of what Dostoevsky's Grand Inquisitor called those'impotent rebels'. While Marx was more optimistic with respect to the amelioration of these conditions than Freud, both rested their case on the therapeutic value of truth. Although this conception of the value of truth has continued in isolated segments of modern secular society, it does not represent the mainstream of this society which tends more and more to exist and survive on varied forms of manufactured opiates, ideological as well as psychological. In this sense the western Enlightenment tradition was fractured first through a process of alienation which helped people conceive of the individual as separate from society and secondly, to conceive that at bottom the search for truth, either in the individual soul or society, was only another illusion. While the former sets the condition for the latter, it is the latter which represents the more profound break in western rationalistic culture.

This break was clearly reflected in the life work of Arthur Schopenhauer (1788-1860) and others who, in the end, found the quest for truth only another illusion. The anti-rationalism of Schopenhauer undercut the enlightenment faith in reason. For Schopenhauer, philosophy ends in silence.[43] Ultimately the illusory phenomenal world is escaped only by a mystical 'turning of the will' against itself as the ascetics and mystics have done throughout history. With the death of personality, Schopenhauer ended his quest in Buddhistic mysticism. Schopenhauer's philosophy of will thus moves into stark pessimism because in the end the search for truth is ultimately only a search through a labyrinth of an illusory phenomenal world. Such a condition makes the quest for truth not only an impossible dream but is ultimately destructive. Thus, Otto Rank, heavily influenced by Schopenhauer, came to the conclusion that the real lesson to be learned from 'Oedipus Rex' was that the search for truth was destructive.

Rank borrowed significantly from Schopenhauer for his understanding of the negative will, the working of the unconscious, the theory of double knowledge we have of ourselves and for his pessimistic, anti-rationalistic view of the world. It was Schopenhauer's theory of the world that Rank discovered behind Richard Wagner's Tristan and Isolde, just as behind Rank's own use of the creative will and his analysis of the creative artist, one can find selected characteristics of the Nietzschean overman.

Rank had drunk deeply from that dark Schopenhauer vessel with its pessimistic romantic nectar brewed in the underworld of strange gods and myth-like creatures which intoxicated so many bourgeoisie at the end of the nineteenth century. Thoroughly alienated from any real sense of effective social action, it was this class which looked within their own souls to find the secrets to the universe. In search for inner authenticity behind the veil of appearances, the brutish world of action could be escaped. In the name of sincerity the Enlightenment values were rejected as illusions. For some, such as Schopenhauer, Rank and others, this quest meant the end of the search for truth which from Socrates on had sustained the western rationalistic mind.

When Rank broke with Freud and made his own psychology explicit, he rejected

Freudian psychoanalysis as too ideological and rationalistic. Rank's psychology was to be based on therapy, not on theory. Denying the importance of the history of the patient in the therapeutic situation, Rank focused his efforts on the immediate present. It was not important, Rank contended, for the patient and the analyst to attempt to discover what really happened because in the end that, too, was illusory. Truth, itself, was purely subjective and relative to what, as Rank put it, 'I want to believe'.[44] To Rank the world of human behaviour is a world of necessary illusions which protect and shield one from seeing the world too well. He believed the neurotic suffered not from living with illusions, but from attempting to live without them. Truth simply robs one of the necessary illusions for living. Rank's therapeutic ideas about 'will therapy' were not only anti-Freudian but fundamentally a denial of the broader Socratic western rationalistic tradition. The good life was to be found not in knowing thyself, but in learning to believe in illusions. Not truth but illusion was his goal of therapy, as he said,

> It is to the effect that our seeking the truth in human motives for acting and thinking is destructive. With the truth, one cannot live. To be able to live one needs illusions, not only outer illusions such as art, religion, philosophy, science and love afford, but inner illusions which first condition the outer. The more a man can take reality as truth, appearance as essence, the sounder, the better adjusted, the happier will he be. At the moment when we begin to search after truth we destroy reality and our relation to it.[45]

Thus, reality itself is illusory. For Rank, self-deception was a necessary condition of life and it was the function of the therapist as a creative artist to enter the world of the patient, making use of transference, to help the individual turn off his over active, negative will which allowed too much truth to destroy his or her illusions and to help the patient to make use of his or her creative will to create effective illusions. It is not the reality behind the displacement that is important, but the displacement itself. To live effectively and to be therapeutically healed is to have learned to live with one's lies.[46] As Rank put it,

> This displacement, if it succeeds, we regard and rightly so as healing, for this constantly effective process of self-deceiving, pretending and blundering, is no psychopathological mechanism, but the essence of reality, the -- as it were -- continuous blunder.[47]

In Rank's 'will therapy' the search for theoretical truths and theory construction to explain behaviour was rejected for a quicker and simpler creation of a patchwork set of illusions with which the patient might live. Under such circumstances it is clear how it was possible for Rank to introduce his therapy as uniquely shortened with a prescribed termination date for the overall process. Although Freud saw this shortened therapy of Rank's as '... designed to accelerate the tempo of analytic therapy to suit the rush to American life ...'[48] and others saw it as an accommodation to modern urban existence, Rank insisted that it was genuinely an integral part of his overall dynamic psychology which was more attuned to modern culture. While Rank, Russell Jacoby[49] and others have repeatedly pointed to the fact that Freud always seemed more interested in theory than therapy, it is not the case that Freud in any ultimate sense could split theory from therapy. For Freud the aim of analytic theory was to discover the truth which was therapeutic. Rank's shift from theory to therapy thus involved not only his distrust of rationalizing about one's past but the very rejection of the search for truth itself and its therapeutic value.

Rank repetitiously argued that Freudian psychoanalysis was ideologically laden in search of universal patterns while his dynamic psychology was concerned with the individual in an assumedly less ideological way.[50] While many of Rank's patients reported his concern for the individual, his involvement in the therapeutic process reflected clear ideological assumptions. One such example was the therapy of Anais Nin. Even though Rank helped Anais Nin discover the 'woman within',[51] she did so by moving rather quickly through Rank's conceptual categories of people. With his help she discovered she was no ordinary woman but rather a creative woman, an artist. Rank believed there were essentially three kinds of people. The lowest kind was, of course, the average man whom he held in low esteem throughout his life. This was the herd that lived and thrived on illusions as reality. The next kind was the neurotic type who is afraid of life; sees too much truth and has difficulty living with his or her illusions because of a negative inverted will. The last kind was the creative artist type that can make use of his or her conscious will to be creative. Fortunately Anais Nin was the latter type.

Thus, Rank categorized people according to their consciousness.

> The average man has reality consciousness more strongly developed, the creative type will consciousness, the neurotic individual self consciousness. Reality consciousness comes from adaptation of will, the creative phantasy consciousness from will affirmation, the neurotic self conscious from will denial.[52]

He conceived these categories as a 'non ideological' description of types which exist within our civilization as a social given. The self-destructive neurotics, he believed, were necessary as a kind of fertilizer of civilization itself. Rank said,

> I think it is the type which we today designate as neurotic which the New Testament characterizes as 'christian' and which Nietzsche in the ideology of earlier times has described as the slave type. These humans who constantly kill themselves, perhaps to escape being sacrificed, need at all events not to be killed any more in order to be utilized as fertilizers of civilization (Kulturdunger, an expression used by Freud who applied it in another connection). In offering themselves up as it were in a Christian sense, they make it not too hard for the others who slay, the lordly natures, the men of will.[53]

What, then, is to be done with these types of people? Are they to be cured of their neurosis so that they, too, might become creative artists like Rank,[54] or are they to be constructively adapted to the 'patient docile Philistine' life which is the 'usual lot of mankind'? Rank went on to say,

> In view of the difficulties of the therapy one must ask whether it is not a vain therapeutic ambition to want to transform this sacrificial type into god-men, and even if this were successful, where shall be forthcoming the necessary hecatombs for the creative type.[55]

The view of the social order, written by Rank in 1929, made up of 'sacrificial types' and 'god-men' or 'creative types' who require sacrificial types for the slaughter in the hecatombs comes strangely close to the social view of fascists who but a few years later were stoking the crematoriums. With this view of the social worder, Rank concluded his discussion of 'will therapy' on a note of adjustment to the inevitable neurotic splits in life, for neurosis itself is part of the creative process of life. Just as Schopenhauer had insisted that a person's character may not change, Rank too insisted,

> The patient must learn to live, to live with his split, his conflict, his ambivalence, which no therapy can take away, for if it could, it would take with it the actual spring of life ... If he only understands how to live in harmony with the inevitable, that is, with the inevitable in himself, not outside, then he will also be able to accept reality as it is. This is no fatalistic and passive acceptance, but rather an active constructive utilization ... In the last analysis therapy can only strive for a new attitude towards the self, a new valuation of it in relation to the past, and a new balancing in relation to and by means of, present reality.[56]

Rank's 'non ideological' view of the social reality toward which adjustment was necessary was the clear recognition that the average man 'needs the external compulsion',[57] the neurotic needs to defend himself against too much external as well as internal compulsion while only the artist as the creative type can 'overcome compulsion through freedom'.[58] The artistic types use the positive will to create ... for itself against the compulsion a reality of its own which makes it independent, but at the same time enables it to live in reality without falling into conflict with it'.[59] This type, while accepting himself and his inner ideal formation, seeks to adjust his environment and others to himself. Sometimes this is done violently as in the case of thoughtless men of action, but it reaches,

> ... its highest level when the individual creates from himself and his own idealized will power, a world for himself, as the artist or the philosopher does, without wanting to force it on others. Certainly this peculiarly creative type also strives for recognition but it cannot as with the therapeutic reformative personality, be through force or violence, but rather must be the expression of a spontaneous movement of the individual who finds in the creator something related to himself.[60]

In the end, Rank saw himself as moving Beyond Psychology, leaving behind all the ideological-oriented psychology, insisting that ultimately there was no logical patterns within the human soul other than what he described in his Will Therapy which he believed was highly individualized and non-ideological. Ultimately he came to the conclusion that his lifelong search 'beyond' individual psychology led him not to a social psychology, but to the '... irrational basis of human nature which lies beyond any psychology, individual or collective'.[61]

IV

Rank's 'will therapy' clearly was not free of ideological assumptions and commitments. His belief in the irrational basis of human nature and the social order with his rejection of the Socratic search for truth and his faith in the therapeutic uses of illusions was founded on a social perspective which not only accepted the injustice and suffering of humanity as necessarily realistic, but which saw the mass of men in terms of 'Pharisees' or slaves with the creative elite alone free of compulsion. All of these ideas fit into Rank's highly ideological view of the world within which he functioned as a therapist.

It was perhaps Rank's social ideology which made him appear so relevant to the psychiatric social workers in America. The exact impact, however, of Rank's work on the field of social work is difficult to determine. On the surface it appears that many of his ideas about reality and illusions might be attractive and highly relevant to the life of the case worker. Fromm's suggestive hypothesis that the effect of Rank's 'will therapy' on social work, placing the problematic blame on the client rather than the social condition and economic structure, ought to be more thoroughly researched and examined than is possible here. A cursory examination of the evidence, however, suggests that Fromm's hypothesis just might be correct. If, for example, Almena Dawley, chief social worker for the Philadelphia Child Guidance Clinic was anywhere near correct when, in her sympathetic eulogy of Rank, she suggested that the effect of Rank's client centered 'will therapy' was to help the social worker to see the need for placing the emphasis of the case worker-client relationship on the 'will' of the client rather than on the content of the 'worker's ideology'[62] then Fromm's hypothesis may have merit.

The problem however is complicated by many factors, not the least of which is the question of how Rank was being interpreted by those who tried to use his therapeutic insights in social work. Some, such as Fay B. Karpf, interpreted both Rank's 'therapeutic approach and general thought' as non-authoritarian as well as client centered. What authoritarian characteristics Karpf found in Rank she attributed to his years of association with Freud and 'other Freudians'. In his post-Freudian years, Karpf believed Rank was non-authoritarian because she found him saying that he believed in '... the equal right of every individual to become and be himself, which actually means to accept his own differences and have it accepted by others'.[63] While it is clear that the authoritarian characteristics implicit in Rank's philosophy and psychology predate and postdate his experiences with Freud, it is equally clear that the 'client centered' therapy espoused and used by Rank was highly authoritarian. While on the surface it may appear that since the mental conditions of all people are believed to be illusory, it might be relatively easy to be client oriented. Unshackled by any authoritative concern for truth, the 'will therapist' could simply help the client adjust to whatever illusions seemed to work. However, once the client entered into the therapeutic process with Rank, he or she was quickly categorized as one of three character types and their corresponding problematic illusory world was as readily interpreted. Rank's short-cut therapy process as described by Anais Nin was, in fact, highly authoritative.[64]

Was Rank then an ideological fascist as Fromm had claimed or was he, as he saw himself, Der Kunstler, who neurotically had seen too much reality, but who through the power of his creative will fashioned his way Beyond Psychology to freedom for himself as well as his patients? In many ways Fromm was correct. Rank had drunk deeply from that wellspring of nineteenth century neo-romantic consciousness which had in the growing crisis of the middle class in the twentieth century become a raging torrent of irrationalism which found expression in modern art, music, literature, religion as well as politics. In this sense, fascism was not an unfortunate accident of the twentieth century, dismissed once and for all by the victory of allied powers in 1945, but rather a political expression of a deeper cultural stream of consciousness which is not readily reversed by the force of arms. While much of Rank's ideology upon which he based his dynamic psychology was similar to, if not the same as many fascist ideologies in the twentieth century, he clearly stopped short of the fascists who advocated the use of force and violence. His was a non-violent if not a friendly fascism. On the other hand, the very conceptual structure of his thought inclined him to think in terms of a large segment of humanity as serving a legitimate function of the hecatombs. If, then, Fromm was correct when he claimed that much of Rank's philosophy which undergirded his psychology was fascist, what is to be made of Fromm's further suggestion that such a philosophy may be nurtured under different symbols and terms?

If fascism is conceived as a political by-product of a deeper cultural and ideological consciousness whose psycho-social origins are transactionally related to the crisis of the middle class and the corporate structure which sustains that class, then it is clear that even though many of the specific historical circumstances that seemed to have triggered some western nations into the political fascism of the 1920s and the 1930s may no longer exist, the underlying stream of irrationalism from which that fascism sprang not only persists but continues to find even more expression in virtually every aspect of modern corporate culture. The failure of our society to develop a more humane political economy, one which lends to young and old alike a sense of worth, dignity and purpose, underlies the decadence of our age. Some seek frantically in such an age to discover their 'roots' in order to overcome their alienated existence and others turn off to life with drugs, alcohol, contemplation, and gurus; others seek escape in the violence of punk rock 'music', the absurdities of Christos' 'art', the psychic-enslavement in Synanon-Moonie type religious cultures, the comforts of the plastic packaged middle class 'Praise the Lord' phenomena or the ultimate sickness unto death in the Jim Jones kind of 'religious' experience. In this sense our art, music and literature, religion, philosophy and psychology profoundly reflect the deeper malaise of the false consciousness emanating from our existentially alienated existence. With Rank we therapeutically embraced this world of consciousness. Under the circumstances it seems understandable why such modern literary artists as Anais Nin and Henry Miller found Rank's sense of reality so appealing.

While the exact impact then of Rank's thought on the field of psychiatric social work remains in doubt, the relevance of Rank's thought as a psychological reflection of the state of much of modern consciousness seems less doubtful. In retrospect, one might ask to what extent Rank's subjective relativistic view of reality and knowledge; his view of truth seeking as not only impossible but destructive; his elitist view of the social order; as well as his therapeutic uses of illusions more accurately reflect the course of western culture than either Marx's or Freud's search for rational truth? The answer to this fateful question might give us some clue as to how far our modern culture has not only adopted a fascist philosophy under different symbols and terms, as Fromm suggested, but also how far modern culture itself has abandoned the Enlightenment vision of both its past and future, and in so doing, has destroyed the rational foundation of its thought.

POSTCRIPT

In writing this paper, I have profited from the critical reactions and dialog of a number of people. I am particularly indebted to Chris Shea for first calling my attention to Rank and doing some of the initial research in this area. I am further indebted to Paul Violas and Jim Anderson for reading and discussion of the paper in its early stages. Lastly, I am heavily in debt to our students in the History of Education program as well as those who participated in both the seminar on 'Fascism' and the seminar on 'Psychological Conceptions of Human Nature' here at the University of Illinois, for their active participation in the dialog out of which many of these ideas were first formulated.

REFERENCES

[1]Erich Fromm. 'The Social Philosophy of Will Therapy', Psychiatry, Vol. 2, May 1939, p. 237.

[2]Ibid., p.237.

[3]In his article, however, Fromm recognized some reservations and indicated that there were certain contradictory elements in Rank's thinking which ran against his analysis, but on the whole, he insisted Rank held a fascist social philosophy, see Ibid., p. 137.

[4]As cited in Jessie Taft, Otto Rank. (New York: The Julian Press, 1958), p. 258.

[5]For an extended analysis of the complicated variety of ways fascism can be viewed, see Walter Laqueur, Fascism: A Reader's Guide. (Berkeley: Univ. of California Press, 1976).

[6]It should be noted that Ernst Nolte was a student of Heidegger in Freiburg during the Third Reich. Heidegger, during those years, was a fascist himself. See Henry Pachter, 'Heidegger and Hitler: The Incompatability of Geist and Politics' Boston University Journal, XXIV3, 1976, Boston, Mass., p.47.

[7]As quoted in Martin Kitchen, 'Ernst Nolte and the Phenomenology of Fascism', Science and Society, Vol. XXXVIII, No. 2, Summer 1974, p. 131.

[8]Ibid., p. 131.

[9]For a particularly insightful critical analysis of Nolte's position, see Ibid.

[10]For example see William Raymond Manchester, The Arms of Krupp (Boston: Little Brown, 1968) and Joseph Borkin, The Crime and Punishment of I. G. Farben. (New York: Macmillan Co., 1978).

[11]Bradford C. Snell, American Ground Transport, Report presented to the subcommittee on Anti-trust and Monopoly of the Committee on the Judiciary United States Senate, Feb. 26, 1974, Government Printing Office, 1974, p.17.

[12]Ibid., p.22.

[13]Ibid., p. 18. It should be noted that the Allies were not able to develop a pure jet aircraft until after the war was over.

[14]Ibid., p.22.

[15]Ibid., p.22.

[16]See Borkin, The Crime and Punishment of I. G. Farben.

[17]There are, for example, some very interesting unexplored similarities over a period of time within this structure. When monopoly capitalism was being consolidated on a national scale at the turn of the century in America and the American liberal state emerged as part of the political-social infra-structure the National Civic Federation was formed which served the interests of big labor, banking, corporations and government by smoothing out their differences so that the overall system might work more effectively. See Gabriel Kolko, The Triumph of Conservatism. (London: Free Press Macmillan, 1963); James Weinstein, The Corporate Ideal in the Liberal State: 1900-1918. (Boston: Beacon Press, 1968); and Robert H. Wiebe, The Search for Order. (New York: Hill and Wang, 1967). In a strikingly similar way today, liberals have attempted to pull together the interests of big labor, banking, multinational corporations and government in the form of the Tri-Lateral Commission, which includes Japan, Western Europe and America to attempt to iron out differences between the three major producing regions of the Western world. The purpose of the Tri-Lateral Commission is similar to that of the National Civic Federation. The difference, of course, is that the NCF was national and the TLC is interational. See Michel J. Crozier, Samuel P. Huntington and Joji Watanuki, The Crisis of Democracy. (New York: New York University Press, 1975).

[18]Dostoevsky, Fyodor, The Brothers Karamazov. (New York: Macmillan Co., 1912) p. 269.

[19]As quoted by Taft, Otto Rank, p.20.

[20]See Ernest Jones, Life and Work of Sigmund Freud, Vol. 2. (New York: Basic Books, 1955), p. 160. Also see Taft, Otto Rank, pp. 3-58.

[21]Taft, Otto Rank, p. 22.

[22]Ibid., p. 15.

[23]Ibid., p. 51.

[24]Ibid., p. 51.

[25]Ibid., p. 52.

[26]Sigmund Freud, Collected Papers, Vol. I. (London: Hogarth Press Ltd., 1953) p. 307.

[27]Gunther Stuhlmann, ed., The Diary of Anais Nin, Vol. I. (New York: Harcourt Brace and World, 1966), p. 279.

[28]That circle then included Rank, Ferenczi, Abraham, Jones, Sachs, and Eitingon.

[29]Otto Rank, Truth and Reality. (New York: W. W. Norton, 1978), p.18. (original copyright date 1929).

[30]For a critical treatment of Rank's behavior during this period (1923-1926) see Ernest Jones, Sigmund Freud Life and Work, Vol. III (London: Hogarth Press, 1957). For a sympathetic account see Taft, Otto Rank, and for a more balanced treatment see Paul Roazen, Freud and His Followers. (New York: Alfred A. Knopf, 1975).

[31]See Roazen, Freud and His Followers, p. 407.

[32]See Jones, Sigmund Freud Life and Work, Vol. III, p. 98.

[33]As quoted by Roazen, Freud and His Followers, p. 418. Roazen also reports that shortly before Freud died Hans Sachs confirmed the fact that in writing this statement Freud had Rank in mind.

[34]Ibid., pp. 408-418.

[35]Jones, Sigmund Freud Life and Work, Vol. III, pp. 59-127.

[36]Taft, Otto Rank, p. 120.

[37]Ibid., p. 120

[38]Marcel Proust's Remembrance of Things Past comes immediately to mind.

[39]For a discussion of these points see Arnold Hauser, The Philosophy of Art History. (New York: World Publishing Co., 1963), p. 62.

[40]It is essentially for these reasons that Marxists such as Arnold Hauser (Ibid., p. 69) and others from the Frankfurt School could attempt to reinterpret Freud within an overall Marxist view of the social order. See Martin Jay, The Dialectical Imagination. (Boston: Little Brown, 1973).

[41]T. B. Bottomore, ed., Karl Marx. (New York: McGraw Hill Book Co., 1956), p. 27.

[42]Sigmund Freud, The Future of an Illusion. (New York: Anchor Books, 1964), p. 92.

[43]It should be noted that another twentieth century philosopher who was deeply influenced by Schopenhauer also ended his thought with a similar pessimistic conclusion. For Schopenhauer's influence on Ludwig Wittgenstein, see G. E. M. Anscombe, Notebook 1914-1916. (Oxford: 1961).

[44]Rank, Truth and Reality, p. 39.

[45]Ibid., p. 42.

[46]See Otto Rank, Will Therapy. (New York: W. W. Norton and Co., 1978), p. 172.

47 Rank, Truth and Reality, p. 42.

48 As quoted by Jones, Sigmund Freud Life and Work, Vol. III, p. 81.

49 See Russell Jacoby, Social Amnesia. (Boston: Beacon Press, 1975).

50 See Rank, Will Therapy, pp. 106-107.

51 Stuhlmann, ed., The Diary of Anais Nin, p.276

52 Rank, Truth and Reality, p. 43.

53 Rank, Will Therapy, p. 200.

54 Rank literally conceived of himself as a creative artist, therapeutically creating people.

55 Rank, Will Therapy, p. 200

56 Ibid., p. 206

57 Rank, Truth and Reality, p. 58

58 Ibid., p. 58.

59 Ibid., p. 58.

60 Ibid., p. 58.

61 Otto Rank, Beyond Psychology. (Camden, N. J.: Haddon Craftsmen, 1941), p. 12.

62 See Almena Dawley, 'Otto Rank's Contribution to Social Work', Social Work Today, January 1940, p. 19.

63 Fay B. Karpf, The Psychology and Psychotherapy of Otto Rank. (New York: Philosophical Library, 1953), p. 16.

64 Stuhlmann, ed., The Diary of Anais Nin, Vol. I, pp. 269-310.

NATURE, NURTURE and POLITICS: A CRITIQUE of the CONVENTIONAL WISDOM

Jonathan Harwood
Lecturer, Department of Liberal Studies in Science
University of Manchester

ABSTRACT

According to the conventional wisdom, the political implications of nature-nurture controversy are straightforward: hereditarian explanations of human behaviour are conducive to 'conservative' politics while environmental explanations encourage 'progressive' politics. Despite the evidence apparently in its favour, the conventional wisdom constitutes a danger for historians by obscuring the contingent character of the connections between nature/nurture and politics. This contingency is demonstrated in two ways. First, attention is drawn to several historical contexts in which hereditarianism was embraced by movements endorsing social reform, and environmentalism was associated with movements opposed to such reform. Second, although the recent controversy in the United States over racial differences in intelligence appears to bear out the conventional wisdom, closer analysis reveals that the hereditarians and their critics <u>share</u> a basic commitment to the meritocracy. Indeed it is precisely this liberal, meritocratic conception of social justice which has fuelled the controversy by attributing political significance to hereditarian and environmentalist theories.

****

In the aftermath of World War Two Nicholas Pastore[1] conducted the first systematic study of the political correlates of the nature-nurture controversy. His conclusions reinforced what has become the conventional post-war wisdom about heredity and environment, a conventional wisdom which has been much in evidence among both participants and commentators in the recent debate over the causes of racial differences in tested intelligence (or 'IQ').[2] According to this view, theories which posit a hereditary cause for individual or group differences in behaviour are seen to favour 'conservative' politics; those which treat such differences as exclusively environmental in origin are thought to be more convenial to 'progressive' politics. As historians working in the shadows of National Socialism and Stalinism, our historiography is particularly at risk. With the Nazis' promotion to hereditarianism from the radical right-wing and Stalin's official sponsorship of Lysenko's environmentalist evolutionary theory from the left firmly engrained in our minds, we are in danger of taking the conventional wisdom for granted. To do so would be to misconstrue the positions of many hereditarians and environmentalists, past and present[3].

In the analysis which follows I will argue that the connections between nature/nurture and politics embodied in the conventional wisdom are historically specific rather than logical in character. The argument is based upon 19th and early 20th century exceptions to the conventional wisdom as well as an analysis of the recent controversy in the United States over racial differences in IQ. This analysis indicates that despite the bitter and politicised character of the controversy since 1969, the hereditarians and their critics differ surprisingly little in their basic political assumptions; only relatively minor questions of social policy have been at stake. Heredity and environment have in fact only become controversial because virtually the entire debate has been conducted within a meritocratic framework which defines nature and nurture as socially significant.

Conservative Environmentalism and Progressive Hereditarianism?

The conventional wisdom described above has not been characteristic of all historical settings. As Charles Rosenberg has shown, medical witnesses for the prosecution in the American 'insanity' trials of the 1880s and 1890s viewed the criminal act as rooted in habits developed in early childhood. Psychiatrists for the defence, in contrast, argued that because criminality was hereditary, the accused could not be held responsible for his actions[4]. In this context environmentalism served to condemn the criminal while hereditarianism exonerated him. The contingent connections between scientific theories and political interpretation can also be seen in the ways in which phrenology was received in the 19th century. That various aspects of human behaviour were thought to be controlled by corresponding regions of the brain was seen as a socially pessimistic form of determinism in Europe. Americans, however, saw in phrenological theory an optimistic doctrine which implied human potential and offered the prospect of the control of personality.[5] Rosenberg portrays the last decades of the 19th century as a crucial period in which programmes of American social reform were gradually uncoupled from hereditarian doctrines and increasingly built upon environmentalist theories.[6]

Nevertheless, twentieth century hereditarianism has not infrequently been associated with various 'socially progressive' political stances varying from social democracy to Marxism. In Britain Cyril Burt and Godfrey Thomson advocated educational selection via intelligence testing in order to extend opportunity to bright working-class children.[7] Between the wars their position was occasionally regarded as 'socialist'.[8] According to Eysenck,[9] Burt voted Labour, read _The New Statesman_, and was seen as a 'pinkie'.[10] In the United States various spokesmen for the reforms of the early 20th century 'Progressive Era' (e.g. Edward Ross, C.H. Cooley, Lester Ward, Herbert Croly) endorsed eugenic measures to some extent.[11] Even such a staunch hereditarian propagandist as Lewis Terman 'maintained an unshakeable commitment to equality of opportunity and social melioration'[12] as well as to the kinds of domestic policies associated in the post-war era with British and Scandinavian Social democracy.[13]

Marxists, too, were not shy of hereditarian ideas between the wars. By 1938 J.B.S. Haldane, for example, had become a declared Marxist and supporter of the Communist Party of Great Britain.[14] In the same year his book _Heredity and Politics_[15] appeared in which he expressed the view that social class differences in IQ were partly genetic in origin.[16] Although he took an agnostic position on racial differences, he admitted finding it 'very hard to rule out nature in explaining differences between Australian aborigines and the Maoris in their ability to assimilate Western culture'.[17] By insisting upon the political _ambiguity_ of biological fact, Haldane was also able, despite his Marxist position, to criticise (in 1940) Lysenkoism, the quasi-environmentalist evolutionary theory which had by then attracted some Soviet authorities' attention.[18]

H. J. Muller, another geneticist who embraced Marxism in the early 1930s,[19] took a very similar position. A convinced eugenist, Muller defended in 1934 orthodox genetics and neo-Darwinian evolutionary theory against the growing attacks then being launched in the Soviet Union by the adherents of Lysenkoism.[20] Only under socialism, he argued, could genetics be correctly applied in eugenics programmes which would serve all mankind.[21,22]

In Germany following World War I, according to Loren Graham, many social democrats and communists supported the eugenics movement.[23] Eugenics thrived as well in the USSR after the Revolution, and Russian scientists debated whether the theory of the inheritance of acquired characteristics had pro- or anti-socialist implications. During the 1920s, however, the German eugenics movement acquired increasingly right-wing, racist associations, a development which inevitably affected the image of eugenics movements elsewhere. In 1930 eugenics in Russia was finished; 'socialist eugenics' had become a contradiction in terms.[24]

When we turn to post-war hereditarianism the data is fragmentary, but the overall picture is similar. Despite the right-wing eugenic fantasies of William Shockley and R. B. Cattell[25] or the apologies for racial segregation in the 1950s and 1960s by Henry Garrett et al.[26], it would be quite inaccurate to brand all post-war hereditarians as reactionary. Of the major spokesmen for the hereditarian position on the race-intelligence controversy since 1969, for example, Herrnstein, Jensen, and Eysenck appear to occupy the broad 'liberal' middle-ground of the British and American political spectra.[27] The central political ideal which guides their perceptions of nature and nurture is that of the 'meritocracy', a political order in which, given equal opportunity, social rank is allocated according to individual merit, and merit consists in large part of inherited intelligence.[28]

Admittedly there is no sense in which Jensen and his supporters could be called 'left-wing'. Significantly, however, the same must be said for the vast majority of Jensen's critics. If one were to take the conventional wisdom for granted it would certainly appear that the recent race-intelligence controversy in the United States was fuelled by the participants' substantially different political orientations; the controversy has been marked by polemic, occasional violence, and frequent reference to the alleged political implications of various positions. And if one looks carefully at their domestic political views, it is true that Jensen's allies and critics disagree over certain relatively limited issues of social policy concerned with the extent of state intervention deemed necessary for ensuring equal opportunity and social justice.[29] Beneath the turbulent surface of the debate, however, lies a very deep and tranquil area of agreement. In their faith in the power of education to alleviate poverty; in their preoccupation with racial rather than social class differences in IQ; and in their assumptions about the social significance of genetic differences in ability, most of Jensen's critics differ very little from his supporters. Both sides' concern for the political significance of heredity and environment derives from their shared commitment to a liberal, meritocratic social order. The extent to which this tacit commitment has structured almost all criticisms of Jensen et al. is usefully illuminated by contrast with the critiques advanced by Richard Lewontin, Christopher Jencks and Noam Chomsky. Starting from various left-radical standpoints,[30] these men, unlike the vast majority of the critics (whom I shall henceforth refer to as 'reformists'), have rejected the conventional wisdom, finding it possible to retain hereditarian theory while discarding the political prescriptions usually derived therefrom.

In the remaining sections of the paper I explore three aspects of the controversy in which the reformist critics' meritocratic liberalism has shaped their response to hereditarianism.

Education and Poverty

In 1964 Lyndon Johnson's Administration introduced a broad package of job-training and compensatory educational programmes for the poor which became known as the 'War on Poverty'.[31] It has often been noted that the War on Poverty stressed education as a solution to poverty.[32] In his educational message to the Congress in 1965 Johnson expressed this succinctly: 'Poverty has many roots, but the tap root is ignorance'.[33] Other cabinet ministers similarly identified the school as a key institution in the attempt to eliminate poverty.[34]

As I have discussed elsewhere,[35] several of Jensen's most eminent critics were social scientists who had made a substantial professional commitment between 1964 and 1968 to various compensatory educational programmes under the War on Poverty, the most famous of which was Project Head Start. Not surprisingly, academics whose research was being subsidised by Head Start were optimistic about education's impact upon social disadvantage. The editors of one conference volume devoted to compensatory educational research observed that subordinate groups had recently begun to seek

> a larger share in the affluence of the society and for the education which will make this possible.[36]

Jensen's reformist critics took the same view. Jane Mercer for example, insisted that it was the school's responsibility to bring minorities into the mainstream of American life.[37] J. McVicker Hunt and Edmund Gordon regarded compensatory education as a way to eliminate the incompetence which produces poverty.[38] Martin Deutsch wrote:

> ... I feel it is only ... through education that disproportionate subgroup concentration in the lower socioeconomic groups can be influenced ...
>
> The school must be a vital institution in the whole process of social change ....[39]

By the late 1960s, confronted with compensatory education's failure to raise IQ or to affect poverty, the reformists cited various technical grounds for this failure: the programmes were poorly organised and underfunded;[40] they sought to improve the wrong class of skills,[41] or they were theoretically underdeveloped.[42] The solution to poverty and related problems, as they saw it, lay in well-designed and executed social policy rather than fundamental structural change. On this point there was no disagreement with Jensen *et al.* As Eysenck maintained, the hereditarians' quarrel with their (reformist) critics concerned means, not ends:

> I agree with the social values of those (critics) who so vehemently disagreed with Jensen (and indeed so does he, of course). Where we part company is in deciding upon the best method for achieving these common aims.[43]

The reformists' faith in education contrasts sharply with the analysis by Jensen's radical critics. From the outset, for example, Jencks was unimpressed:

> ... the most conspicuous fact about the (War on Poverty) is that it consists almost entirely of old programs aimed at traditional objects; the elimination not of poverty but of ignorance, incompetence and so forth. The problem may have been redefined but the solutions have not.

> (This) fundamentally conservative (programme) assumed that the poor are poor not because the economy is mismanaged but because the poor themselves have something wrong with them ... They have the wrong skills ... and won't enroll in training programs. They have too little education and won't go back to school.[44]

In Inequality[45] Jencks and collaborators later launched a full-scale attack upon the belief that education was an important source of economic inequality in the United States and were, predictably, attacked in turn by reformists such as Martin Deutsch.[46]

Preoccupation with Racial Differences

One of the interesting features of the controversy since 1969 has been the extent to which the reformist (and lay) response to Jensen et al. has been largely confined to racial differences in IQ, addressing the issue of social class differences comparatively rarely. This selective response is no doubt due in part to the fact that the Civil Rights movement of the early 1960s and the black nationalist movements of the late 1960s were still major political issues at the time Jensen and Herrnstein published their controversial claims. Furthermore the hypothesis that social class differences in IQ are partially genetic in origin is probably empirically stronger than the racial hypothesis. Nevertheless the social class hypothesis was hardly invincible; data were then available which could have been used to argue that the magnitude of innate class differences was so small as to be economically negligible.[47] That most critics nevertheless failed to exploit this possibility suggests that they found the social class hypothesis far less disturbing than the racial one. The background to the publication and reception of Herrnstein's article 'IQ'[48] supports this interpretation.

When Herrnstein first submitted his manuscript to the editors of Atlantic Monthly they thought it was

> too dull; not provocative enough ... Someone at the Atlantic called it 'soporific' ... too academic.
>
> ... The people at Atlantic had wanted me to talk more about race differences, and I resisted the pressure to do so.[49]

Most of the eventual published version of the paper was devoted to substantiating Herrnstein's central argument that if (1) differences in mental abilities are inherited, (2) success requires those abilities, and (3) earnings and prestige depend on success, then social standing will be based to some extent on inherited differences among people; in short, the meritocratic ideal. Only 1½ of the essay's 16 pages discussed racial differences in IQ, and on that issue Herrnstein took an agnostic position. After outlining Jensen's hypothesis, he concluded:

> Although there are scraps of evidence for a genetic component in the back-white difference, the overwhelming case is for believing that American blacks have been at an environmental disadvantage ... a neutral commentator ... would have to say that the case is simply not settled, given our present stage of knowledge.[50]

This was evidently not controversial enough for the Atlantic Monthly editors for in their long introduction to 'IQ' each of their five paragraphs mentioned racial differences.

The editors seem to have judged the sensitivities of their readership well. Supplemented with this misleading introduction, the September 1971 issue, bearing a giant 'IQ' on the cover, was sold out all over the United States within a few days. Despite Herrnstein's reluctance to draw firm conclusions on the race-IQ issue, a number of the newspaper accounts and criticisms of 'IQ' focussed on race differences.[51] Similarly a few months later Atlantic Monthly published a sampling of the 'scores of letters' they had received in response to the article.[52] Of the 28 published letters - most of them criticisms from academics - fully a quarter of them focused on the race-IQ issue, taking Herrnstein to task for claims he hadn't made.[53]

As Bowles and Gintis have observed, what debate has occurred between hereditarians and their reformist critics over the significance of social class differences in IQ

> ... has been curiously superficial: the putative economic importance of IQ has remained undocumented by the genetic school and unchallenged by their critics.[54]

That mental ability (whether measured by IQ or other tests) is a scarce, essential commodity in modern societies which must therefore be unequally rewarded is simply taken for granted by hereditarians as well as their reformist critics.

Again it is instructive to compare the reformists' response to that of the radical critics. Chomsky has been one of the few critics to identify and attack the meritocratic premises underlying Herrnstein's position.[55] Similarly Jencks et al. have granted that a part of the average black-white difference in IQ may be genetic but have insisted that this fact, even if established, would be of slight economic significance in contemporary society[56] compared to class differences:

> It seems quite shocking ... that white workers earn 50% more than black workers. But we are even more disturbed by the fact that the best paid fifth of all white workers earns 600% more than the worst-paid fifth. ...
>
> We would, of course, like to see a society in which everyone's opportunities for advancement were equal. But we are far more interested in a society where the extremes of wealth and poverty are entirely eliminated than in a society where they are merely uncorrelated with skin color, economic origins, sex and other such traits.[57]

The Implications of Genetic Differences

It is quite clear that Jensen's major reformist critics endorse the meritocratic ideal. Dobzhansky, for example, regards meritocracy as 'almost necessarily the outcome' of the equality of opportunity which he endorses.[58] Although Hunt thought the 'spectre' of a genetically stratified society rather less imminent than Herrnstein claimed, he saw

> a fair degree of force in the (argument) ... it has a ring of truth in it.[59]

Martin Deutsch's assumptions about the social order are no less evident:

> Of course, in the broadest sense, the objective is to assist children in the realization of individual potential leading to the jumping of social class boundaries. The eventual aim

> of school integration, thought of in this social context, is to eliminate the largely ethnic bias of social class membership and to create conditions in which basic ability will be the determinant of social mobility ...[60]

It is thus not very surprising that neither Dobzhansky[61], Deutsch[62], nor Hunt[63] were particularly enthusiastic about Jencks'[64] suggestion that the solution to poverty lies not in educational reform but in major income redistribution. Nor is it surprising that most critics concentrated their fire on the issue of racial rather than social class differences in IQ.

For the meritocrat genetic inequality is the backbone of a just social order. Any criterion of merit which varies substantially for environmental reasons is an imperfect criterion. It implies that social conditions have not been equivalent for all competitors; true equality of opportunity will require some kind of compensatory social or educational reform so that an individual's reward will be strictly proportional to his or her 'true' (i.e. - genetically rather than environmentally based) merit. Thus reformists cannot accept a genetic component to racial differences in IQ because on meritocratic logic this would necessitate fewer class-based advantages on average for blacks than for whites, a consequence which seems to violate many reformists' conception of racial equality and integration.[65] As Edgar Z. Friedenberg has noted

> ... by acknowledging Jensen's paper as damaging to (black aspirations), one must, in effect, acknowledge the value of the social system and its structure of rewards.[66]

The debate since 1969 therefore *appears* to reinforce the conventional wisdom concerning nature/nurture and politics because it has been conducted almost entirely within a meritocratic framework by American liberals who are undecided whether equality of opportunity *has* (e.g. Jensen *et al.*) or has *not* (e.g. reformist critics) yet been satisfactorily achieved.[67]

Starting from a different conception of social justice, on the other hand, some radical critics have been able to accept the possibility of genetic differences without accepting the meritocratic implications which both hereditarians and reformist critics have taken for granted. Chomsky, for example, grants that individual differences may be largely genetic but denies that society must consequently evolve classes with different levels of ability.[68] Lewontin, too, is un-dismayed by genetic differences in ability:

> ... suppose the difference between black and white IQ distributions were completely genetic: what program for social action flows from that fact? ... whether those differences are genetical, maternal, obstetrical or Oedipal, the decision about what role each child is to play eventually in society and what rewards he will receive is social.[69]

Thus the enormously *controversial* character of heredity versus environment has arisen out of virtually unexamined and *uncontroversial* political premises.

CONCLUSION

The basic idea in the foregoing argument is not new. It has not only been prefigured, for example, in Charles Rosenberg's and Loren Graham's work but also in recent analyses of early 20th century American nature-nurture controversy. Clarence Karier has argued that the American environmentalist Lester Ward and the hereditarian Edward L. Thorndike differed not over whether society should be governed by intellect but only over whether it already was being so governed.[70] Russell Marks has interpreted the famous debate over IQ testing between Lewis Terman and Walter Lippmann in the 1920s as a policy debate within the liberalism of the time.[71] [72] In their attacks upon the liberal supporters of the War on Poverty, William Ryan[73] and Stanley Aronowitz recognised several features of what I have called the reformists' position:

> ... the liberals who assert their adherence to equality are constrained by their own acceptance of the prevailing social division of labour and the role of IQ measures, public schools and merit within it. Too often they share the conservative belief that incremental changes can remedy the illnesses of society and only differ with them about the pace and extent of these changes.[74]

My intention here has been twofold: (a) to extend these insights to the recent race-intelligence controversy and (b) to develop the historiographic implications of such evidence: if the political significance attributed to nature and nurture is context-dependent, then historians must be wary of using uncritically the conventional wisdom of the present to interpret the past.

Much work remains to be done. One of the weaknesses of my argument is that although I have shown that the connections between nature/nurture and politics are context-dependent, I am unable to explain convincingly how these connections have been forged or why they change. It is important to identify the precise circumstances - whether in late 19th century America, in Germany during the 1920s, or in post-war Britain - in which particular political movements came to perceive hereditarian or environmentalist doctrines as potentially useful (or threatening).[75] Eysenck, for example, informs us that his political allegiance has shifted since the 1930s from Marxism to socialism to liberalism.[76] How typical was it for British hereditarian-meritocrats to affiliate to the Labour Party before the war, joining the Black Paperite wing of the Tories thereafter? Did this correspond to a general drift to the Left by the Conservative Party promoted by the Depression, the war and the Beveridge Report, thus obliging Labour to develop a strategy based on environmentalism and comprehensivization since the 1950s?[77] Perhaps these particular questions are misconceived; I am in any case unable to answer them. But in my view these are the kinds of questions about political context which we will have to ask in order to understand the origins of the current conventional wisdom.

****

I would like to thank David Hamilton, Clarence Karier, Richard Lewontin, Donald Mackenzie, Gary Werskey and Edward Yoxen for commenting on an earlier draft of this paper.

REFERENCES

[1]N. Pastore, The Nature-Nurture Controversy (New York: Kings Cross Press, 1949).

[2]Cf. J. J. Harwood, 'The Race-Intelligence Controversy: a Sociological Approach II - "External Factors"', Social Studies of Science Vol. 7 (1977), 5-7.

[3]Nicholas Pastore's classic book clearly illustrates the dangers of the conventional wisdom. He treats nature/nurture and political positions as consonant or

contradictory (180), thus creating for himself a series of awkward anomalies. For example he finds it necessary to treat Karl Pearson prior to 1900 as a 'socialist environmentalist' but in his later career as a 'conservative hereditarian'. Donald Mackenzie, on the other hand, unconstrained by the conventional wisdom, has stressed the continuity in Pearson's Fabian Socialist-hereditarianism before and after 1900 (D. Mackenzie, 'Karl Pearson and the Professional Middle Class', Annals of Science, Vol. 36 (1979), 136). Faced with Lewis Terman's hereditarianism yet strong social democratic political sympathies after World War II, Pastore is forced to classify Terman as an unexplained exception to the rule (94-95). Similar difficulties arise with the radical H. J. Muller whom Pastore classifies as an 'environmentalist' despite the fact that Muller went so far as to accept the likelihood of genetically based racial differences in mental traits (UNESCO, The Race Concept: Results of an Inquiry (Paris: UNESCO, 1952), 52-55). Muller thoroughly rejected being classified as either environmentalist or hereditarian (Pastore, 155) for reasons which the rest of this paper should make clear. Pastore runs into the same difficulty by classifying the one-time Communist J.B.S. Haldane as an 'environmentalist' while acknowledging Haldane's belief in a genetic contribution to intelligence differences between social classes (Pastore, 168-9).

[4] C. Rosenberg, 'Scientific Theories and Social Thought' in B. Barnes (ed.) Sociology of Science (Harmondsworth:Penguin, 1972), 299-300.

[5] Ibid., 301.

[6] C. Rosenberg, 'The Bitter Fruit: Heredity, Disease and Social Thought in Nineteenth Century America', Perspectives in American History Vol. 8 (1974), 189-235.

[7] On Burt see Gillian Sutherland and Stephen Sharp, '"The Fust Official Psychologist in the Wurrld" : Aspects of the Professionalisation of Psychology in Early 20th Century Britain', History of Science, forthcoming. On Thomson see H.M. Paterson, 'Godfrey Thomson and the Development of Psychometrics in Scotland 1925-1950', unpublished paper, Department of Education, University of Glasgow, 1975. At the conference from which this book emerged several participants offered anecdotal evidence which supports my characterization of inter-war British psychometrics. Stanley Nisbet, a student of Thomson's in the 1930s, pointed out that W. McClelland was another tester at Moray House College of Education who tried to assist able but disadvantaged children by assessing mental ability in a 'disinterested' way. Robert Bell, whose extensive research on Godfrey Thomson is as yet unpublished (cf. his 'Godfrey Thomson and Scottish Education', unpublished paper, 1975, Faculty of Educational Studies, The Open University), noted that Thomson's work was admired by various figures on the Left such as Jenny Lee.

[8] Gillian Sutherland, 'The Magic of Measurement: Mental Testing and English Education 1900-1940', Transactions of the Royal Historical Society, Vol. 27, 5th series (1977), 148.

[9] Interview, 17 December 1974.

[10] In his Cyril Burt: Psychologist (London: Hodder and Soughton, 1979) L.S. Hearnshaw substantiates Eysencks' impressions. Neither Burt's published work nor unpublished papers give any indication that he wished to defend the 'Establishment' (61); if anything he inclined to make fun of it (267). Though toward the end of his life he rejected both major parties and never voted at elections, he was enthusiastic about the Beveridge Report and was knighted by a Labour government (127). In Hearnshaw's judgement Burt is best characterised as 'left-of-centre'.

[11]On Ross and Cooley see, for example, Paul Violas 'Progressive Social Philosophy: Charles Horton Cooley and Edward Alsworth Ross' in C. Karier, P. Violas and J. Spring, Roots of Crisis (Chicago: Rand-McNally, 1973), 40-65. On Croly see D. Pickens, Eugenics and The Progressives (Nashville, Tennessee: Vanderbilt UP, 1968), 111. On Ward see C. Karier, Shaping The American Educational State (New York: Free Press, 1975), 194-5.

[12]Russell Marks, 'Lewis M. Terman: Individual Differences and The Construction of Social Reality', Educational Theory, Vol. 24 (1979), 336.

[13]Pastore, op cit., 94-95.

[14]Gary Werskey, The Visible College (London: Allen Lane, 1978), 158.

[15]London: Allen and Unwin, 1938.

[16]Ibid., 116.

[17]Ibid., 131.

[18]Werskey, op cit., 294.

[19]Garland Allen, 'Science and Society in the Eugenic Thought of H.J. Muller', Bioscience, Vol. 20, No. 6 (1970), 350-51.

[20]H. J. Muller, 'Lenin's Doctrines in Relation to Genetics' in To the Memory of V. I. Lenin (Moscow, 1934); reprinted in Loren Graham, Science and Philosophy in the Soviet Union (New York: Knopf, 1972), 453-69.

[21]Ibid., 466-68.

[22]It seems to me that some historical work on the eugenics movement has suffered from the conventional wisdom, though this is more evident in matters of emphasis than of fact. For example while acknowledging the existence of a vocal group of socialists within the British eugenics movement in the 1930s, G.R. Searle ('Eugenics and Politics in Britain in the 1930s', Annals of Science, Vol. 36 (1979), 159-69) repeatedly characterises the movement as a whole as 'conservative' without explaining what 'conservative' then meant. This omission is compounded by referring to R.B. Cattell as a 'right-wing extremist', a label which is appropriate in the political spectrum of the 1970s but which ignores Cattell's admiration for the socialism of Shaw and Wells in the 1920s and 1930s (cf. his autobiographies in G. Lindzey (ed.) The History of Psychology in Autobiography, Vol. 6 (New York: Prentice Hall, 1974) and in T.S. Krawiec (ed.) The Psychologists, Vol. 2 (New York: Oxford University Press, 1974)).

[23]Loren Graham, 'Science and Values: the Eugenics Movement in Germany and Russia in the 1920s', American Historical Review, Vol. 82 (1977), 1140-44.

[24]Ibid., 1146-56.

[25]A New Morality from Science: Beyondism (Elmsford, New York: Pergamon, 1972).

[26]See, for example, Charles Silberman, Crisis in Black and White (London: Jonathan Cape, 1965), 257-58.

[27]In a letter to me dated 4 May 1977 Herrnstein said that he generally votes for the candidate furthest to the left. His guess was that Jensen was more likely to vote Democratic than Republican. Eysenck strongly rejects the label 'right-of-centre', and professes to be thoroughly disillusioned with both Conservative and Labour Parties (letter to me dated 23 February 1976).

[28]Cf. Harwood 1977 op cit.; Harwood, 'The Race-Intelligence Controversy: a Sociological Approach I - Professional Factors', Social Studies of Science, Vol. 6 (1976), 380-81, 392; and Harwood, 'Heredity, Environment and the Legitimation of Social Policy' in B. Barnes and S. Shapin (eds.) Natural Order

(London: Sage, 1979), 231-51.

[29]See Harwood 1979. Of course Jensen's supporters, unlike his critics, have strongly opposed what they regard as the 'reverse discrimination' of compensatory education and the Affirmative Action programme (Harwood 1976, 380-81). Nevertheless reformist critics are no more sympathetic in principle to 'reverse discrimination' than are Jensen et al. since it violates meritocratic principles. For reformists these programmes did not 'discriminate' in favour of blacks so much as 'equalise opportunity' for them.

[30]Lewontin is a professed Marxist and Chomsky, a 'libertarian socialist' (see his 'Comments on Herrnstein's Response', Cognition, Vol. 1, No. 3 (1972), reprinted in N. J. Block and G. Dworkin (eds.) The IQ Controversy (New York: Pantheon Books, 1976), 318). To classify Jencks as a 'radical' may seem somewhat dubious in view of his argument that one of the major causes of economic inequality in the United States was 'luck' (Jencks et al. Inequality (New York: Harper & Row, 1973), 226-7). He has, however, more recently admitted that this was a serious error (A.H. Halsey, 'Introduction', in A. H. Halsey (ed.) Heredity and Environment (London: Methuen, 1977), 23), and G. Hodgson ('Do Schools Make a Difference?' Atlantic Monthly (February 1973), 46), has referred to Jencks' 'New Left leanings'. Jencks himself says that he left the Washington social policy scene in 1967, convinced that the liberal social reforms of the 1960s had been predicated on a false analysis of the nature of poverty. ('Inequality in Retrospect', Harvard Educational Review, Vol. 43, No. 1 (1973), 138-64). He came to reject the ethics of reward being proportional to productivity and to dismiss the possibility of substantial social reform by equalizing educational opportunity. The only solution to economic inequality, he concluded, was 'socialism', namely 'political control over the economic institutions that shape our society' (Inequality, 265). Thus I have no evidence to suggest that Jencks is a Marxist, but presumably he would be welcome, say, on the left-wing of today's Labour Party.

[31]D. P. Moynihan, Maximum Feasible Misunderstanding (New York: Free Press, 1969); P. Marris and M. Rein, Dilemmas of Social Reform (London: Routledge and Kegan Paul, 1967); S. Levitan, The Great Society's Poor Law (Baltimore: Johns Hopkins UP, 1969).

[32]E.g. H. Aaron, Politics and the Professors (Washington: Brookings Institution, 1978); Marris and Rein, op cit., 16.

[33]Cited in M. Katz (ed.) School Reform: Past and Present (Boston: Little-Brown, 1974), 24-26.

[34]P. Meranto, The Politics of Federal Aid to Education (New York: Syracuse UP, 1967), 36.

[35]'Knowledge, Credibility and Social Change: American Nature-Nurture Controversy since 1960', unpublished paper, 1980.

[36]B. S. Bloom, A. Davis and R. Hess (eds.), Compensatory Education for Cultural Deprivation (New York: Holt, Rinehart and Winston, 1965), 2; see also p.5. In Deprivation and Compensatory Education (New York: Houghton Mifflin, 1968) Helen Rees expressed the same view: 'It is ... essential that we see education as the enemy of poverty, for it must be through education that the deprived successfully work their way toward better conditions'. (156).

[37]J. R. Mercer and W. C. Brown, 'Racial Differences in IQ: Fact or Artifact?' in Carl Senna (ed.) The Fallacy of IQ (New York: Third Press-J. Okpaku, 1973), 108.

[38] J. McV. Hunt, The Challenge of Incompetence and Poverty (Champaign-Urbana, Illinois: University of Illinois Press, 1969), viii; E. Gordon, 'Some theoretical and Practical Problems in Compensatory Education as an Antidote to Poverty' in V.L. Allen (ed.) Psychological Factors in Poverty (Chicago: Markham, 1970), 322-23. In recent years Gordon has abandoned this optimism for a more radical analysis of poverty; see his 'New Perspectives on Old Issues in Education for the Minority Poor', IRCD Bulletin, Vol. 10, No. 1 (Winter 1975), 16.

[39] These two quotes are taken from M. Deutsch et al., The Disadvantaged Child (New York: Basic Books, 1967), 281 and 282, respectively. Similar expressions of faith in the power of education to bring about social progress are made by various reformist critics in the spring 1966 issue of American Child and in A. H. Passow (ed.) Education in Depressed Areas (New York: Teachers' College Press, 1963).

[40] M. and C. Deutsch, 'Intelligence, Heredity and Environment: The Critical Appraisal of an Outmoded Controversy', New York University Education Quarterly (Winter 1974), 4-12.

[41] Gordon in Allen, op cit., 1970, 322.

[42] Hunt, op cit., 1969.

[43] H. J. Eysenck Race, Intelligence and Education (London: Temple Smith, 1971), 152. See also his 'When is Discrimination?' in C. B. Cox and R. Boyson (eds.) Black Paper 1977 (London: Temple Smith, 1977), 96.

[44] These two quotes are taken from Necks, 'Johnson versus Poverty' New Republic, Vol. 150 (28 March 1964), 15 and 18 respectively.

[45] New York: Harper and Row, 1973.

[46] Deutsch and Deutsch, 1974.

[47] That individual differences in IQ are to some substantial degree heritable and that various social classes and racial groups differ in average IQ are two reasonably well-established building blocks of the hereditarians' social class and racial hypotheses. The racial hypothesis, however, is seriously weakened by the fact that it is not known whether environmental differences between black and white populations are comparable to those within the white population (for a general discussion see J. C. Loehlin, G. Lindzey and J.N. Spuhler, Race Differences in Intelligence (San Francisco: W. H. Freeman, 1975)). The social class hypothesis, by contrast, appears more convincing at this point partly because social class differences in performance persist even on IQ test items which seem devoid of all class-cultural bias (e.g. K. Eells et al. Intelligence and Cultural Differences (Chicago: University of Chicago Press, 1951), esp. Chapter 7). More importantly the main thrust of the hereditarian argument was not simply that IQ differences between classes are genetic but that IQ was the major determinant of an individual's class position. It was, therefore, crucial to the hereditarians' hypothesis that children of higher IQ are upwardly mobile while those of lower IQ move down in the social hierarchy. Apart from the continuing American popular belief in the Horatio Alger myth, there was in fact some published evidence on this point which was available while the controversy was at its peak (reviewed in Loehlin et al., 167-68. The reported correlation between IQ and social mobility, however, was a modest one. For example where sons' IQs were between 8 and 23 points higher than their fathers', almost three-quarters of the sons retained their fathers' social status or were downwardly mobile (J. H. Waller, 'Achievement and Social Mobility: Relationships among IQ Score, Education and Occupation in Two Generations', Social Biology, Vol. 18 (1971), 252-59). The fathers'

occupation was just as good a predictor of their sons' occupational level as was the sons' IQ. Accordingly Waller was only able to conclude that social status in his sample was 'in some degree' attributable to IQ. In a similar vein the Robbins Report had noted in 1963 that substantially fewer higher-IQ working-class children ended up in higher education than did high-IQ middle-class children. Still more damaging to the hereditarians' social class hypothesis were the analyses by Bowles (summarised in S. Bowles and H. Gintis, Schooling in Capitalist America (London: Routledge and Kegan Paul, 1976), 119-22 and by Jencks et al. (Inequality, 188, 220-21), showing that IQ differences are far less important than class background or educational status or, even more strikingly, income. Thus the most vulnerable part of the hereditarian hypothesis concerned the alleged economic importance of IQ and its equation with social success.

[48]Atlantic Monthly (September 1971), 43-64.

[49]Interview with Herrnstein, 6 June 1974.

[50]'IQ', Atlantic Monthly (September 1971), 57.

[51]Herrnstein in interview plus his IQ in the Meritocracy (Boston: Little-Brown, 1973), 161.

[52]'More about IQ', Atlantic Monthly (December 1971), 101-110.

[53]By contrast when one of Herrnstein's students sought support among Harvard staff and students for his critique of Herrnstein's social class hypothesis, he encountered general apathy. (George Purvin, 'Introduction to Herrnstein 101', Social Policy (July-August, 1973), 76-87). That the involvement of genes in social class differences in IQ was not especially controversial to the reformists in the late 1960s can also be seen from a typical reformist book: M. Deutsch, I. Katz and A. R. Jensen (eds.) Social Class, Race and Psychological Development (New York: Holt, Rinehart and Winston, 1968). Containing papers by Deutsch, Hunt and Gordon along with various others which argue that racial differences in the test scores are environmental in origin, the lead essay nevertheless declares social class differences in IQ to be partly genetic at present and increasingly so in future.

[54]S. Bowles and H. Gintis, op cit., 116.

[55]The exchange between Herrnstein and Chomsky has been reprinted in Block and Dworkin, 285-324.

[56]Jencks et al., 72, 83.

[57]Ibid., 14.

[58]Th. Dobzhansky, 'Is Genetic Diversity Compatible with Human Equality?' Social Biology, Vol. 20, No. 3 (1973), 280-88.

[59]Interview with Hunt, 26 June 1974.

[60]Deutsch et al., 1967, 294 (emphasis mine); cf. 281.

[61]Dobzhansky, op cit.; cf. his Genetic Diversity and Human Equality (New York: Basic Books, 1973).

[62]Interview with Deutsch, 13 June 1974.

[63]Interview.

[64]Inequality.

[65]It remains unclear why the reformists' conception of racial integration should differ from that of the hereditarians. In earlier work I have been more successful in characterising these differing models of integration than in explaining their origins (Harwood 1977, 1979).

[66]'The New Assault on Equality: a Symposium', Social Policy (March/April 1973), 56.

[67]I am very much aware of having appeared to conflate the political motives of the major academic participants in the race-IQ controversy with the actual political consequences of hereditarianism and environmentalism in contemporary society; e.g. Jensen and Eysenck may be liberals, but the members of the National Front and the White Citizens' Council are not. Such an objection to my argument would be justified on the basis of the limited evidence I have presented here. Elsewhere, however, I have argued that quite apart from the motives of Jensen and his critics, the controversy over racial differences in IQ has been closely tied (at least in the United States) to a debate within contemporary liberalism over alternative strategies for the management of racial unrest (Harwood, 1979).

[68]In Block and Dworkin, op cit.

[69]'Further remarks on Race and the Genetics of Intelligence', Bulletin of the Atomic Scientists, Vol. 25 (May 1970), 25; see also his 'Biological Determinism as a Social Weapon' in Ann Arbor Science for the People (eds.) Biology as a Social Weapon (Mineapolis, Minnesota: Burgess, 1977), 8.

[70]Shaping the American Educational State, 197.

[71]Russell Marks, 'Testers, Trackers and Trustees: The Ideology of the Intelligence Testing Movement in America, 1900-1945', Ph.D. dissertation, University of Illinois, 1972, 144-52. His 'Race and Immigration: The Politics of Intelligence Testers' (in Karier, ibid., 316-342) is the first serious attempt to situate various phases of the race-intelligence controversy in their social context and has influenced my own thinking substantially.

[72]Gary Werskey has also contributed to this line of argument in suggesting that disagreement between environmentalists and eugenists as to the causes of poverty in Britain prior to World War I was confined to debating the merits of alternative forms of biological engineering, both couched within the same political perspective: 'social imperialism' (The Visible College, 29-30).

[73]Blaming the Victim (New York: Pantheon, 1971), esp. 6, 7, 24.

[74]'The Trap of Environmentalism', Social Policy (September-October 1972), 36.

[75]Throughout the paper I have used the labels 'progressive', 'conservative', 'socialist' etc. without definition, attempting only to convey roughly the political associations of nature and nurture as historical actors have perceived them. Because the meaning of political labels changes, however, it may be objected that what I have documented here are not changing perceptions of nature and nurture but the drift of the political centre: e.g. the meritocratic implications of hereditarianism might be the same now as fifty years ago, but meritocratic policies have moved from left to right. Some of the historical data (from Britain for example) may fit this interpretation, but it seems on the other hand very unlikely, for example, that those socialists in the 1920s and 1930s who accepted eugenic principles were any more right-wing than contemporary socialists who almost invariably reject such principles. Furthermore on logical grounds hereditarian and environmentalist theories do not specify unique political consequences. A meritocratic system could confer the greatest rewards upon those who make the most sacrifices for the community (the capacity for self-sacrifice being presumably equally distributed among all persons). Alternatively the mere existence of genetic differences in mental ability does not preclude special help for the disadvantaged; to provide (or refuse) such help is a political decision.

[76]'The Dangers of the New Zealots', Encounter (December 1972), 79.

[77]Although it makes no reference to nature/nurture, a promising analysis along these lines is D. Finn, N. Grant and R. Johnson, 'Education, Social Democracy and the Crisis', Cultural Studies, Vol. 10 (1977)

AFTERWORD

The purpose of this afterword is two-fold. First, to indicate the coherence of the foregoing collection of papers; and second, to point to some of the areas that might merit closer examination in the future.

The contributors to this volume can be divided into two groups. On the one hand there are those who view educational research from an outside vantage point (e.g. the history of science) and, on the other hand, there are those who look at it self-consciously, as educationists of one complexion or another. In another sense, however, these two constituencies come together in their readiness to treat the conduct of educational inquiry as problematic: a historically- and philosophically-located form of social practice.

There is a certain irony in this last position since it was the 'scientific' movement that originally toppled history (of a certain kind) from its position as queen of the educational sciences in the beginning of the twentieth century. The preface to one of the earliest textbooks used in the training of teachers - R. M. Quick's Essays on Educational Reformers (1869) - maintained that 'practical men in education' would derive substantial benefit from the study of 'what has already been said and done' in that field. Yet, by the publication of Bain's Education as a Science, the practical basis of education was deemed to rest upon the 'principles furnished by the several sciences involved' and upon the 'statement, deduction and proof of the various maxims or rules that make up the art'.

The papers in this volume, then, display some of the various forms taken by educational inquiry over the last century. Perhaps the most striking feature to emerge is the evidence - from a variety of sources - of the strong influence of German social thought (in the form of metaphysics and idealism) upon the twentieth-century Anglo-Saxon social sciences. The full story remains to be told but it seems the case that the popular conception that empiricism replaced (and effaced) idealism is no longer tenable. In short, the distance from Herbart to Mach and from Wundt to Freud is much less than conventionally imagined. Indeed, at a very superficial level all these thinkers espoused and advanced psychologistic (or psycho-physical) forms of explanation - ideas which prefigured much that subsequently passed as educational research.

The full social and historical significance of these developments (e.g. their relationship to forms of life as well as forms of thought in capitalist societies) is only slowly being understood.

As the papers suggest, the stream of culture that nurtures educational research has survived relatively unchanged. Its 'progressive' qualities, nonetheless, have been challenged, both from within and without. At one extreme there has been a utopian rejection of educational research (which is usually based on a confusion of science with empiricism); while at the other extreme, there have been attempts to meet the problems of empiricism by generating 'more of the same' (e.g. the development of multi-dimensional forms of simple regression analysis). Intellectually, the net result is stalemate - a dialogue of the deaf. Socially, the dominant ideas retain their ascendency and thus confirm the status quo.

We believe that historical analysis points the way towards resolution of this deadlock; while accepting the need for disciplined enquiry, it cannot afford to accept the boundaries between the various disciplines of enquiry as given, a priori. To return to our original division of the participants at the seminar; the educationists were concerned with the authenticity of practice whereas the historians were interested in its historicity. These are not separate questions since authenticity, like historicity, is about the relationship between action and context. An understanding of these relationships is central to the advancement of both educational and historical inquiry. Whether or not philosophical analysis 'leaves everything as it is' - as many of its exponents have claimed - historical analysis certainly does not.

Considered from the vantage point of the late twentieth century, the history of educational research is largely the history of mental testing and experimental design. Certainly, a prominent place must be found for these in the historical record. Nonetheless, other domains, now perhaps forgotten, must receive their due. Even a cursory investigation of early educational journals suggests a new array of topics. What importance, for instance, should be attached to the Child Study movement? What role did the school health service play in the dissemination of the experimental method (e.g. through studies conducted in the 1920s to assess the efficacy of school milk)? Did formal research play any part in the spread of 'progressive' ideas in primary education between the two World Wars? What have been the changing fortunes of research into teaching?

Besides these substantive topics, there are also a number of recurrent issues in the history of ideas that deserve attention. What counted as 'proof' in the days before randomisation and the controlled experiment? What part has 'research methods' played in the training of teachers? What has been the relationship between educational inquiry and the so-called 'contributory' disciplines? What has been the evolving link between educational research and social policy?

Finally, there is an important constellation of issues in the social history (or the social relations) of science. When, where and why did the educational research community emerge? What were its sources of legitimation? What role has been played by the British Psychological Society in moulding the careers of educational researchers? What part did the Scottish B.Ed. (now the M.Ed.) play in the growth of mental testing in England? Who were the mavericks in educational research? And why?

Set against this list, the papers in the volume merely constitute a preliminary sampler. They raise as many questions as they answer. Yet, as in a sampler, their strength is perhaps in the range of styles that they display and the possibilities that they foreshadow.

****

INDEX